ACCLAIM FOR "T...

"The expression *faith can move mountains* was coined for people like her."

—DIANNE WATTS
MAYOR, SURREY, BC

"I know that if it wasn't for her support and her believing in me until I could believe in myself I wouldn't be alive today."

—KRISTY WILSON

MaryAnne openly shares her journey as a reluctant but willing recruit into the purposes of God in her life. She asks the question, "How much is one life worth?" As you read through these pages, you cannot help but feel the prodding of the Spirit of God asking you the same question and demanding your own heart to respond. I highly recommend this book to you. Let it open your eyes and heart to the stark reality that everyone is in desperate need of a Saviour, and everyone deserves to be rescued.

—HELEN BURNS, PASTOR
RELATE CHURCH

"A genuine book of a miracle! Buy this book. Read this book. Then look and listen for God's voice so you can create your own miracle."

the SHIFT

'Be 'Shifted'
With Love
Grace &

Sph 3: 16-20

the SHIFT

The Power of Belief

MARYANNE CONNOR

Published by Shift Publishing and printed in Canada by Printorium Bookworks.

All net profits of the sale of this book (after costs of printing, editing, and distribution) are donated by the author to NightShift Street Ministries Society, a not-for-profit Christian organization, headquartered at 10635 King George Blvd., Surrey, British Columbia, Canada, V3T 2X6.

Cover design by Tony Mitchell, Original Mix Design

ISBN 978-0-9939773-0-5

DEDICATION

To my Papa,
You're the One my heart is spoken for!
I love You, Lord!

—Isaiah 61:1-4

CONTENTS

PREFACE

WHAT BEGAN IN A SNOWSTORM in 2004 has grown into a movement to alleviate poverty and rescue lost souls from our meanest streets.

The original edition of The Shift: The Power Of Belief helped people recognize the desperate circumstances of 'the least of us' and the problems involved in establishing, maintaining and broadening the services of NightShift Street Ministries. The book inspired many people to donate, tithe and volunteer, and their generosity is acknowledged and greatly appreciated. It has saved and rescued lives.

But there is still much to be done to complete God's work and the ministry's vision.

This new, revised edition of The Shift takes readers a step deeper into a personal and spiritual understanding of the issues you and I and our society cannot avoid as Christians and caring people – for this is clearly ours to do.

The revised edition includes a Discussion Guide to encourage personal self-exploration and the exchange of ideas in church study groups, business clubs and readers clubs. The Guide is designed to challenge you – your beliefs in God, your understanding of self, your surprising connections with those less fortunate.

Many people who read the original edition of The Shift have asked

- What can I do to help?

- What does the volunteer service require?

- Are there age restrictions?

- Do I have to be a church member?

- Is there any way I can learn more without obligation?

On the What Now section at the back of the book, the new, revised edition clearly defines what services NightShift offers, how to participate, including the regular Info Nights where you may visit without obligation and learn exactly what is required of volunteers.

You'll also find a Prayer of Surrender, an opportunity to surrender yourself to the Power of Jesus Christ.

The edition also includes photographs that document the joy and salvation that NightShift Street Ministries and our volunteers bring to the streets every single night of the year, as well as the breadth of professional services the organization offers.

Finally, this new edition offers a lovely and inspirational gift.

It is a song by the artist, Kelita, who was inspired to write Embrace The Shift after reading the first edition of The Shift: The Power of Belief. She wrote the lyrics and music and presented the song as a surprise at the ministry's 2013 December Gala of Light. Needless to say, we were overwhelmed by her heartfelt message. At the end pages of this edition, you will find how to download the song from iTunes with partial profits directed to NightShift.

Thank you for your continuing support of our organization.

God bless you.

—MaryAnne Connor

FOREWORD

I ADMIRE PEOPLE of faith who live their beliefs in non-violent and inspiring ways.

When I was younger and travelling across Europe and Asia for a couple of years with a knapsack on my back, I came across a lot of different people with strongly held beliefs about the meaning of existence and the power of faith.

The experience made it clear to me that my own spiritual beliefs—true and comforting as they are to me—were not necessarily shared by the majority of the rest of the world. I could choose to decide that others' faiths were wrong, or misguided, or even quaint—or I could accept that faith was a personal choice, as valid as my own.

I decided on the latter.

The decision has served me well as mayor of one of the most diverse ethnic communities in Canada.

I found that honouring the faith of other religions only served to strengthen my personal beliefs. My faith in my understanding of God was not diminished by watching someone else pray to or celebrate different concepts of the Almighty. Quite the opposite. I saw that in spite of whatever cultural and historic differences there might be, we shared a belief in a Supreme Being, which was a common bond.

Some people truly take that to heart, which brings me to MaryAnne Connor and her creation, NightShift Street Ministries. Her faith in God—or Papa, as she calls Him in this book—has *shifted* her from being a woman anxious and frightened around the homeless to their loving and compassionate champion.

NightShift began seven years ago in Whalley, Surrey's inner city beset by the homeless. What started as a portable soup kitchen (with a lot of listening, hand-holding and prayer circles) has grown to becoming a fully realized and professionally administered recovery program for street people with addictions. For that to have happened required many people demonstrating their faith and a consider-able amount of *shifting*—including, it must be said, the administration of the City of Surrey.

MaryAnne's book records many of the obstacles NightShift had to overcome simply to exist and operate on our city streets. She discusses this frankly, including some surprising obstacles—*spears*, as she calls them—pitched by church leaders in her own Christian community.

What I find so moving about her story is her absolute faith in God. Time and again, when the odds are stacked against her, Papa gives her the energy and fortitude to persevere. A little like Tevye from the musical *Fiddler On The Roof,* MaryAnne communicates with God. He leads her, most often through Bible passages, to new understandings about herself and the situations she encounters.

In other words, He *shifts* her.

Not that she and I always agree about the city's public policies, and in fact sometimes she can be disagreeable. (I'm not comparing her to Mother Teresa but neither do I ever remember reading that Mother Teresa was always agreeable.) However, my same personal and professional experience with MaryAnne (now Reverend Connor) informs me that she is devout. The expression "Faith can move mountains" was coined for people like her.

I realize that not everyone is convinced about faith based charities. Some argue that in spite of the obvious good work NightShift performs every night—rain or snow, 365 nights of the year—feeding and clothing the least fortunate of us, critical to its mission is to preach the Word of God. Proselytizing, those critics would say, questioning the legitimacy of this service in an otherwise officially secular social service system.

My response is two-fold. First, well-run, reliable faith-based services like NightShift provide unquestionably necessary services—in this case for the poor and home-less—that city and provincial agencies simply couldn't afford to staff and maintain, and these services are delivered not impartially or bureaucratically but with love, a rare commodity, something that no amount of taxpayer dollars can provide.

Second, the central presence of God in the NightShift program is precisely what the drug- and alcohol-addicted need for their recovery. Integral to virtually all recovery programs—particularly the proven 12-Step Alcoholics Anonymous (AA) program and similar 12-step programs for cocaine, heroin, meth, and other drug addictions—is the presence and belief in a Higher Power.

Through prayer, care counselling, and considerable patience, NightShift has brought addicts off the street, into recovery homes and programs, and ultimately back to our community. As it continues to expand its reach and services, the organization, now with its own recovery program, promises to bring even more souls back from their imprisonment in addiction.

And all this, it should be noted, with virtually no taxpayer funding.

Much has *shifted* over the first seven years of NightShift's existence, including the city's recognition and appreciation of volunteerism and faith-based community services that are now integral to the city's social planning. (My goodness, MaryAnne even became a member of the Whalley Business Improvement Association, the same WBIA with which she had had so much conflict.)

Volunteers unite our city and enrich our lives. Unquestionably, we accomplish more through collaboration. Together with our neighbours, volunteers create a stronger, more productive community.

NightShift, with its 2,500 subscribers who tithe their time, money, prayers, and gifts-in-kind, is a shining example of volunteerism, the power of people, and their ability to shape the future.

May God bless them.

—**Dianne Watts**
Mayor, City of Surrey, British Columbia 2012

Chapter 1

SNOWSTORM

I DIDN'T WANT the pastor to drop the church key into my hand. I didn't want to be in charge of the prostitutes and pimps, drug dealers and addicts who'd come into church to stay overnight to get out of the storm. Homeless people frightened me. I didn't know what to say to them. I certainly didn't want to touch them.

Please, I am just a tiny, blonde lady in nail polish and lip-gloss. I like going to spas and nice lunches. I was getting over a failed marriage; I was trying to reboot my real estate marketing company. I was to address the National Association of Home Builders (NAHB) Builders' Show in Las Vegas about how to increase profits. I was trying to become America's leading real estate marketing consultant and get my own cable show. And now I was in a decaying street mission that smelled of wet clothes and unwashed derelicts, with the filthiest washroom in Whalley that reeked of urine and feces (I could barely step in there), with more and more scary people—many of them armed with knives—coming in the church doors. I didn't want this. I wanted my broken life back. I wanted to be in my little rented cottage in upscale White Rock. Safe. And warm.

Well, not so warm.

That's how it started.

It was January 2004 and a sudden onset of winter had hit the normally balmy British Columbia coast. Dense, heavy, cold air occupied valleys and coastal inlets and dropped temperatures to minus 20°C in places. Vancouver dipped to minus 12.2°C with a wind that made it feel like minus 20°C, the coldest day in seven years. It was one super-sized, super-charged arctic air mass that punished the coast with every conceivable type of severe winter condition: raging blizzards, freezing rain, piles of snow, numbing wind chill, black ice, flash freezes, and sustained bouts of severe cold.

One night during the storm, I tiptoed across the icy floor of my bedroom in my bare feet to the bathroom. Angry gusts of wind, blowing snow, and arctic air blasted the sides of my much-loved but ancient cottage. The thin walls trembled. Windows shook. I dove back under the covers, pulled my soft feather duvet over my head, and settled back into the warmth of my comfy bed. I rolled over sleepily and settled back into my dream.

Seconds later, eyes wide open, frustrated, my thoughts turned to the street. This was going to be one of those nights. Sleepless.

Where are they sleeping tonight?

The homeless, just thirty minutes away on the streets of Whalley, the City of Surrey's inner city.

I flipped to the other side. Dug down deeper.

There are people out there without a roof over their heads. In this atrocious weather! That's just wrong.

Yes, I know, I answered my thoughts, but I was cozy.

"God, please let me sleep!" I pleaded.

I rolled back on my back and stared up at the ceiling.

"Somebody should do something."

My heart skipped a beat. Awkward silence. Weakly, I whispered, "Was that someone me, God?"

My bed was becoming not so snug.

In spite of the insane weather, the next morning I ventured out to church, a safe distance from my cottage. Following the service, I chatted with a guy who had a heart for those who were struggling with addictions on the street. I'd had some experience working with charities that served the poor and homeless, but always on the board level or as an entrepreneur whose real estate promotions had raised money for various causes. I felt drawn to serving the homeless but I'd always kept myself safely away from actual contact. I never got my hands dirty

Our discussion centered on us approaching Pastor Steen at the Gentle Shepherd Church to ask him about opening the doors of his church for homeless people in Whalley to give them somewhere safe to sleep for the duration of the storm. I agreed to make the trip, but really I wasn't keen about doing it. Driving twenty-two kilometres on my own in such severe weather conditions was probably not a smart thing to do, but before I could back out, I climbed into my car and headed to Whalley.

The roads were treacherous. Blinding snow. Ice pellets stuck on my windshield. Wipers rendered useless. Black ice. I barely missed the car in front of me. *Honkin' big angels must be on duty,* I thought. *What am I doing?* My heart hammered in my chest. Adrenaline rushed to the tips of my toes. I muttered under my breath, through clenched teeth, "I'm turning back. This is crazy."

But I kept going. The entire time I argued with God and myself about whether I should be going to Whalley in the first place. What was I thinking? As usual, I hadn't been thinking at all, and reflecting back, if I had, I probably wouldn't have made the trek.

I entered the church building to find Pastor Steen busy preaching to a small gathering of street people, huddled together drinking hot coffee and munching on donuts. The musty stench of wet clothes mingled with body odour almost made my stomach retch. I squeezed my way through to where people stood in line for more coffee, elbowed my way to the back of the makeshift kitchen area, where I found Pastor Steen's right-hand man, and proceeded to present him with my great idea. Let me tell you: Steen's right-hand guy will never win Mr. Congeniality. Without regard to my enthusiasm or goodwill, he cut me off, said my idea stank, and told me in no uncertain terms that Pastor Steen would never agree to open the church after hours. Scowling, he turned his back and told me to go home, lady.

I was crushed.

I was also thoroughly confused because I was pretty sure I had heard from God about pursuing this idea. Apparently, I had made a mistake. My death-defying trip through the storm had been a huge waste of time.

Discouraged, I found a space at the back wall and listened to Pastor Steen finish delivering his message. As the prayer came to a close, he caught my eye and pushed his way through the small crowd to say hello. He was surprised to see me on a Sunday afternoon, especially during this grievous weather. As we chatted, two small words whispered gently to my spirit, "Ask him."

My heart fluttered. I had a genuine fear of Mr. Congeniality in the kitchen. Going over his head wasn't a wise thing to do. I ignored the whisper and focused on my conversation with Pastor Steen. Within seconds, I heard the whisper a second time, "Ask him," spoken this time with more urgency. I could see Mr. Congeniality over Pastor Steen's shoulder. I still prickled from his stinging rebuke. Once again I ignored the prompt. Almost immediately, I heard the third whisper, spoken this time with a sense of authority. "Ask him." Before I could question any further, I interrupted Pastor Steen mid-sentence and blurted, "Pastor Steen, forgive me for interrupting, but I need to ask you something really important."

With one eye on the guy in the kitchen, I asked Pastor Steen if he would consider opening his church so that people on the street would have a place to lay their heads that night. He looked at me thoughtfully and said, "I think that might be something we could consider. I'll bring this up at our board meeting next week."

Before I could lose my nerve, I continued pressing, "But Pastor, the need is now. The storm is raging today. You need to open the church tonight!"

What I didn't know was that Pastor Steen and his wife, Lyn, had found a homeless man sleeping under the stairwell of their apartment building that very morning. They thought perhaps they should be doing something to help those on the street during the storm. However, Steen's health was failing and they were not in a position to open the church overnight on their own.

Here's the thing: that morning they had asked God to send someone to help.

Enter me—the innocent lamb.

Steen glanced at Lyn. Without comment, he dug deep into his pocket and did an unexpected thing. He dropped a set of keys into my hand. Then he spoke words I will never forget. "I'll open the doors of the church tonight, but on one condition—you're responsible."

I can't describe the panic that gripped my heart. Reverse! Back up the bus! Sure, I thought it was a good idea, but never in my wildest dreams did I think it was a good idea for me to do the job. I had said, "*You* need to open the church." I didn't say, "*I* need to open the church!"

What had I done? No, let me rephrase that. What had God done?

My drive back home to White Rock was an emotional nightmare. How did I get myself into such a mess? Talk about "open mouth and insert foot!" I was acutely aware that I was in way over my head. I didn't have a clue how to run a shelter. Especially a shelter for people who terrified me! I recalled John Ortberg's book *If You Want to Walk on Water, You Have to Get Out of the Boat* about stepping out of your comfort zone. Stepping out of your comfort zone? This was crazy! This was stepping out off a cliff!

It was getting late and I didn't have much time to prepare, so I did the only thing I knew how to do. I cried for help! I cried tears too and, thankfully, friends responded. By the time I headed back to Whalley a few hours later, my car was jammed with blankets and sleeping bags. As a backup, I paid the first of what would become many visits to a local food store. I piled a grocery cart full of everything I could think of to get us through that first night—bread, peanut butter, jelly, cookies, juice, milk, and tons of sugar. People living on the street love sugar! Heaps of it!

In the meantime, I had given the church keys to a guy who had responded to my cry for help and who had agreed to wait at the church in case anyone showed up to volunteer before I got there. When I arrived, I walked through the front door—to complete chaos. The church was dark and packed with people. Cigarette smoke hung thickly in the air; the impact almost knocked me over. In shock, confused about what was happening, I found my way to the back of the church. This was God's house, not a place for people to hang out all night and smoke cigarettes. Pastor Steen had given me authority to look after his church. I had agreed to step into that role, whether I liked it or not. So I stepped forward.

I wasn't very popular that night or for many nights afterwards. There was a split opinion on how the shelter should run. I chose to lead with love while others led with an iron fist—but there would be rules. No swearing, no knives or weapons, no smoking, no drugs to be used in the church or the church washroom. I was a small, blonde woman who was scared of the dark in more ways than one. But here I was in spite of myself: God had placed me in charge. There was much push-back, but I was determined to respect God and to direct the shelter as He led me. Order was restored.

I will never forget that first night. A small number of people from the church I attended came along, headed up by a friend who agreed to help. I took kitchen duty, if you could call it a kitchen, and got the coffee urn ready. Thirty-five people shuffled through the door. One after the other, they had appeared seemingly led by the Holy Spirit's prompting. No one had told them the church was opening its doors, yet they arrived in all shapes and sizes—exhausted, shivering cold, soaking wet, ravenously hungry, coughing and spewing—in various states of despair and disarray. As I witnessed the unsightly procession staggering in, I fought to overcome my fear.

We worked quickly to provide a place on the floor, which was covered by a thin layer of dirty outdoor carpet. There were no mats or beds, but people were grateful for a blanket and a warm place to lay their head for the night, protected from the raging storm outside. Soon the never-ending line-up for coffee and sandwiches began. While the guys handled the heavy work of moving chairs and distributing blankets, I sprang into action in the kitchen, where I was safe. The serving window separated me from the crowd. I introduced myself, asking for the names of people while I served them hot coffee and stacks of thick peanut-butter-and-jelly sandwiches.

I remember the people I met that first night. People whom at that time I called prostitutes, addicts, criminals, drug dealers, and pimps. Pain and heartache were etched on every face. Faces that still run through my mind like a scene from a movie. My heart broke over and over again as I began to hear their stories. I remained on my side of the window, ensuring my safety was intact, and talked through the wee hours of the night. Slowly I forgot my fear as my heart connected with theirs and theirs with mine. I fell in love with people who I discovered were no different from me. As the night continued, my passion for business and my former lifestyle slowly began to ebb away.

"Forgetting what is behind and straining toward to what is ahead, I press on toward the goal to win the prize to which God has called me …" (Phil. 3.13 NIV).

Before lights out, as people were bedding down, we prayed a children's bedtime prayer, "Now I lay me down to sleep …" I was astonished. Almost every person in that room sat up in their makeshift beds and joined us in the prayer. I'm not sure what shook me most—that they responded to receiving prayer, or that most of them knew it.

During the night, I prayed over people as they lay sleeping on the floor. I was surprised and deeply moved by the peacefulness I saw settle on their sleeping faces. Regardless of their individual reasons for being here—it didn't matter if they were roughened criminals or drug dealers, sex-trade workers, or people just trying to stay alive in hardship—they were here, safe and warm in a place where they felt loved. It was as if we were tucking children in for the night. My heart swelled as I saw women curled up snuggling teddy bears.

This could have been me, or perhaps one of my children. There, but by the grace of God, go I.

It was during this week-long snowstorm that I first began to understand what Jesus meant when He said, "Truly I tell you, whatever you did for one of the least of these brothers and sisters of mine, you did for me" (Matt. 25:40 NIV).

It was the Call. I was surrendering to God.

DISCUSSION QUESTIONS

1. **Do you feel called?**
   - What calls you?
   - What motivates you?

2. **God speaks to us in many ways—in our quiet moments or by moving us to tears.**
   - Do you listen?
   - How do you respond?

3. **What is your snowstorm?**
   - What has been your 'snowstorm' moment when you felt moved enough to speak out or do something to make a difference in your life or the lives of others?

4. **Have you ever done something that was way out of your comfort zone?**
   - What did you do?
   - How did you feel?
   - Did you feel God's presence alongside you?
   - What did you learn about yourself?

5. **Can you find love again?**
   - Where do you look for love?

Chapter 2

WHY US?

WHY ME? YOU may have asked that yourself a few times. Why were you the one who was always the caregiver? Why were you the one diagnosed? Why were you saved when someone else wasn't? Why you? Why me? Why us?

I don't have an answer, of course. God hasn't chosen to spell out His divine plan to me. But I should warn you: at the risk of sounding flakey, I speak to God—and about God—all the time. God and I are tight. We chat. When I say, "I hear from Him," or "God said," I don't mean that I hear the rumble of His audible voice. Nor does He visit me looking like George Burns or Morgan Freeman, as in the movies.

Generally, when I spend time with God, studying His Word, the Holy Spirit shows me something. I might get a thought or a whisper pressed into my heart. Or feel goose bumps—I call them God-bumps. Maybe the hair stands up on my arms. I might cry like a baby. Sometimes my legs get heavy. I know that might sound odd, but that's what I feel when God comes around or—if you prefer—when God comes upon me.

Sometimes I catch a hint of a word. One or two at the most. On rare occasions, a short phrase. I know for sure it didn't come from me because it doesn't sound like something I would say or think. I test it. Wait for confirmation in some way. If He's adamant, He'll repeat it three times. By the third time, I sit up and pay attention.

Some people say only weak people need God. Today I'd say they are absolutely right. Call me weak. I would have adamantly fought you on that when I was living in the Fall, depending on myself without God, like Adam and Eve when they were expelled from the Garden of Eden for not listening to God about eating fruit from the Tree of Life. I was a survivor dependent only on myself. Proud and strong. Determined. Back then, "weak" was not a word in my vocabulary. But in reality, I am weak. And now I realize weak is a good thing.

It brings me to the end of myself. It stops the incessant brawl with myself, others, and God. Let go. Let God. Yes! Like the Buddhist proverb says, "When the student is ready, the teacher appears." Die to self. Open to God. The Bible, the ultimate authority, says, "That is why, for Christ's sake, I delight in weaknesses, in insults, in hardships, in persecutions, in difficulties. For when I am weak, then I am strong" (2 Cor. 12:10 NIV).

Why me? I don't know. Like many of you, I've done a lot of work to get here. Well, it's truer to say God has done a lot of work to get me here, but here we are. Maybe you are too—just ready to *shift*. To enter a new phase of your life. To start seeing life from outside the box, as the current jargon goes.

In my case, at first I didn't know why God chose a woman like me to start a ministry. But He did. That I can no longer deny. I struggled with accepting this for a long time—why me?—until I finally got it by reading the many stories in the Bible that reveal how God has always used ordinary, fallen people. Moses—not that I presume to compare myself with this great prophet and Jewish saviour, but we both had trouble speaking. He was a stutterer; I get so anxious before speaking I'm often in tears (Ex. 4:10). David had an affair and was a murderer (2 Sam. 11:27); Mary Magdalene was delivered from seven demons (Mark 16:9); Rahab was a prostitute (Josh. 2:1); the Samaritan woman at the well had five husbands (John 4:18); and countless others like them had notable failings, but God still chose them to accomplish His divine purposes. So in wonder and awe, I've humbly come to accept that His glorious line-up includes failed people like me—and perhaps people like you.

For as long as I can remember, I've had an entrepreneurial spirit percolating inside me. In my early teens, I started my own business teaching ballet and later moved on to pursue some rather interesting career choices. Self-employed for most of my career, I've enjoyed the fruit of my labour. I owned and operated The Connor Group Real Estate Marketing Inc., a small real estate agency and marketing firm in Vancouver, British Columbia, Canada, from 1997 to 2004. Before that, I spent twenty years in business and real estate development in eastern and western Canada and owned and operated two successful model and talent agencies on the East Coast.

During those years, I judged many housing awards across the country and was fortunate to be the recipient of a few. Whenever possible, I was always involved on the boards of business community organizations such as the South Fraser Child Development Centre Fundraising Committee and the Greater Vancouver Home Builders' Association.

I've always been passionate about businesses giving back to the community and was constantly devising sales and marketing campaigns to raise money for charities. Every opportunity I could find, I'd merge my builder clients' sales and marketing programs with media, public relations, and promotional events to sell their new home communities while raising public awareness and money for a good cause. They were a win/win for everyone.

In 1997, the Every Woman's Dream Home raised $100,000 for breast cancer research. In 2000, the Z-95 Give-Away Sticker campaign, a huge radio promotion, raised support and tremendous community recognition for the South Fraser Child Development Centre. In 2002, Everyman's Dream Home raised $100,000 for prostate cancer research. These events were some of the highlights of my career.

When God stirred my heart in those days with God-things that weren't business related, I often wondered why He was asking me to do this in the midst of my busy career. In looking back, I see that He had a purpose and was methodically putting the plan in place for my life and what was ultimately to become NightShift. While I worked on achieving my business goals, God slowly turned my heart to a healing ministry. He had deposited into my heart an intense hunger to know Him more. It has never ceased. A passion for a counselling and prayer ministry came with that hunger, which sent me searching and devouring every book I could find on these topics.

God opened the door to Burden Bearers of Canada in 1988 when I first sought out Christian counselling during a stressful time in my life. I eventually served as a Burden Bearers board member, received basic counsellor training, and facilitated a Women's 12-Step Program. My pursuit for personal healing broadened with Listening Prayer Community, where God began the gruelling process of setting me free through week-long intensive listening prayer sessions. It was at Listening Prayer that I received solid prayer ministry training. This transformed my personal walk and eventually formed the foundation for NightShift's counselling ministry.

I accepted a board position as vice president with Lifeline Outreach Society, a mobile soup kitchen and food bank that served the homeless in downtown Vancouver. It was at Lifeline where I received my first taste of street ministry. Although deeply touched by Lifeline's mission, I had no desire to get my hands dirty by serving the poor and homeless. Instead I created their branding and spearheaded their fundraising initiatives. I was convinced that helping the homeless on the front line wasn't my gift. Surely God wanted me to make tons of money while I enjoyed the fringe benefits and gave a percentage to worthwhile charities, didn't He?

By 1999, all I had striven for in my life was coming unglued. Although my business goals and aspirations were falling into place, my personal life was screwed up. My third marriage was falling apart. It became more and more of a challenge to hide behind the shield of my business success and to put on my "happy face" mask.

The final straw came with 9/11.

Like the rest of the world, I watched in horror as the tragedy unfolded on television. Like many others, this event proved to be a turning point in my life. Something had shifted in my spirit during that time of grief and loss. Deep in my heart, I knew I was perishing myself, struggling with pain and grief deeply imbedded in my soul. The pain began to surface, leak, and spill over the constraints of my heart.

"I see you!"

The words were spoken over me in prayer following a gruelling week-long Listening Prayer Training. I was in a very fragile state. My life was crumbling before me. Starved for nourishment, I splashed those living words over my thirsty heart. It was comforting to know that God sees me! The God of the universe, Creator of all things, sees my pain and me! What a beautiful thing to say and just at the right time. As I prepared to leave, one of the worship leaders approached me saying, "Wasn't that great? God sees you!"

Before I could reply, my spirit saw three letters. ICU. The worship leader continued speaking. She asked, "I wonder what He meant?"

In a heartbeat, I knew. I saw a picture of me in an intensive care unit (ICU). "I see you." Her words were prophetic because, unknown to me, I was just about to step into a virtual operating room—for surgery on my broken heart.

What I'm about to tell you next represents a huge leap of faith for me. I can't explain how God healed my life without personal disclosure and transparency. I feel like I'm about to roll down the zipper of myself to let you peek inside. I know I run the risk of being misunderstood and misjudged.

Perhaps any one of us—exposed—would feel anxious. My life is messy. I've hidden truths and tried to minimize the impact of negative events, my way of getting through difficult times, always pretending I was okay. Vulnerability is not my favourite means of expression.

Nor am I keen on sharing with others my intimacy with God. Like revealing a secret, sharing this union with Him somehow diminishes its richness, but He has asked me to do this. I wish to be a good daughter. I am doing what my Papa asks.

DISCUSSION QUESTIONS

1. **How does God speak to you?**
   - What thought or whisper has been pressed into your heart?
   - What word or phrase?

2. **What does it mean to you to "let go, let God?"**

3. **Have you ever felt 'goose bumps' that feel like 'God-bumps'?**
   - Describe the experience.
   - How did you respond to it or why did you ignore it?
   - What do you think it meant?

4. **Is God asking you to get your hands dirty?**
   - How does this make you feel?

Chapter 3

PAIN

THE DICTIONARY DESCRIBES pain as "ache, sting, throbbing, grief, sorrow, anguish, and agony." That perfectly described mine. By spring 2002, my emotional pain had become so unbearable that I suffered extreme migraine headaches and chronic physical pain. In desperation, I revved up my counselling sessions and suffered through several trial marriage separations, trying to save a marriage rapidly falling apart. But by then it was too late. After much prayer and seeking God's will, I left our beautiful house boat, my life there, and moved, for a six-month season, to a tiny rental cottage in White Rock, a small seaside community on the British Columbia Lower Mainland near the U.S./Canada border.

My husband and I agreed to continue individual counselling and work on our marriage from a distance. After six months, my husband had moved on. With a broken heart, I moved on, too. Living alone, for the first time in my life.

I left my marriage with nothing, not even my Gracie, our beloved two-year-old golden retriever. She stayed behind to comfort my husband. Items gathered from garage sales slowly turned my sparse two-room cottage into a temporary home. Over time, I scraped up the remnants of my life and started the process of gluing together the shattered pieces.

I didn't think I was broken. Denial was my stronghold and my enemy.

My usual remedy for the pain was work and crazy busyness, but this time God wouldn't allow it. He pushed the pause button and forced me to wrestle with the reality of my fear of being alone. God spoke, "For God did not give us a spirit of fear but a spirit of power, love, and a sound mind" (2 Timothy 1:7 NKJV); and "There is no fear in love. But perfect love drives out fear, because fear has to do with punishment. The one who fears is not made perfect in love" (1 John 4:18 NIV).

He wanted to show me what perfect love looked like. I hung on to these scriptures like my very life depended on it. I spent hours in prayer and devotion. God showed me I had run into relationships to ward off my fear of being alone, a soul sickness that had haunted me for as long as I could remember. He revealed to me the shame and self-blame I put upon myself for being a failure, a horrible wife, and a terrible mother. A profound sadness began to wrap around me like a heavy coat.

As the days dragged on, my coat got heavier. Already I had come through a lifetime of fear and pain. Loss, grief, and loneliness had been my constant companions since the death of my father early in my fourteenth year. Two years later, I became pregnant with my first child, forcing me into the unexpected role of a teenage wife and mother. Ten years later, at age twenty-six, I suffered the loss of my third child during my seventh month of pregnancy, and a year later, heartache all over again from the murder of my first husband. These were undoubtedly the most painful years of my life. My three companions—Loss, Pain, and Loneliness—were faithful as they continued with me through the dysfunction and final collapse of my second marriage of thirteen years. And now, here was the death of the third marriage. My three surviving children, whose hearts were broken with mine, struggled with a mother constantly caught in survival mode.

There were times I didn't want to wake up to face another day. Isolation became my coping tool. I was convinced there was no one to turn to; such was the state of my depression. I spent hours alone looking out at the ocean or gazing up at the stars from my rooftop deck. Finally, exhausted from fighting loneliness and fear, I turned to the only One who could save me from my broken heart. And, as always, He stood close by. In the early days, someone had told me there was beauty beyond pain. Blinded by pain, I couldn't see beyond. Over and over again, God spoke, "Weeping is for a night but joy cometh in the morning ... you turned my wailing into dancing, you removed my sackcloth and clothed me with joy" (Ps. 30:5, 11 NIV).

As the months continued, I began to journal. As my tears fell, the pages filled. The Lord began to reveal things to me and about me. He spoke to me about trust, courage, pain, and faith. I knew in my heart that this time things were going to be different. No longer was He allowing me to run from my pain into yet another dysfunctional relationship or to hide behind busyness. I remember it as if it were yesterday, standing in front of my window overlooking the ocean, my heart aching so much that I had difficulty breathing. He told me to "embrace" the pain—to turn into it, not run from it. He said it wasn't going to kill me, even though it felt like it would. Then He asked me to do the impossible. Trust Him. Trust Him to bring me through the pain.

The hurt was so acute, making it impossible to fall back into familiar denial patterns. I felt paralyzed. Walls of protection wrapped around me so thick they were impossible to penetrate, even by me. My strongholds. "The weapons we fight with are not the weapons of the world. On the contrary, they have divine power to demolish strongholds" (2 Cor. 10:4 NIV).

The Lord wanted them removed. Slowly, He began to teach me what surrender looked like. He began to remove the strongholds that kept me frozen. Day by day, I came to realize that life wasn't all about me. Slowly, as I came to this realization, I began to come to the end of myself. I began to trust God to show me another way.

God could only start the healing process in my life when I faced the truth of myself. He's gentle. He waited until I was willing to let go. Let go. Let God in. "The truth will set you free" (John 8:32 NIV).

God grant me serenity.

The walls began to crumble when I moved into the safety of His love. As I did, my heart began to heal. Day by day, He brought me to deeper depths and greater heights. As I surrendered, He began to breathe life and joy into my heart. Josh Wilson's "Before the Morning" lyrics beautifully describe "beauty beyond the pain."

> 'Cause the pain that you've been feeling
> It can't compare to the joy that's coming
> 'Cause the pain that you've been feeling
> It's just the hurt before the healing
> 'Cause the pain that you've been feeling
> It's just the dark before the morning
> Once you feel the weight of glory
> All your pain will fade to memory

Years before, my youngest daughter had left me a beautiful note with a scripture God had given her to bless me on one of my dark nights. God highlighted this scripture once again through an amazing allegorical novel written by Hannah Hurnard, *Hinds' Feet On High Places*. I was very much like "Much-Afraid," the girl in that story. Our lives paralleled. God had brought her through depths of pain, fear, and loneliness to greater heights in Him. Now He was doing the same for me.

> Though the fig tree does not bud and there are no grapes on the vines, though the olive crop fails and the fields produce no food, though there are no sheep in the pen and no cattle in the stalls, yet I will rejoice in the Lord, I will be joyful in God my Saviour. The Sovereign Lord is my strength; he makes my feet like the feet of the deer; he enables me to go on the heights.
>
> —Habakkuk 3:17-19 NIV

God nudged my heart again to encourage me to venture further out of my familiar threshold. My pastor preached a message, "Putting God First in Your Life," and I was certain his message was directed right at me. If I were truthful with myself, I hadn't been placing God first in my life in any area. In fact, I had left Him at the altar to pursue wrong relationships and money without His blessing. I now made the decision to place God "first" in my life. I began to see the pain and needs of others rather than always focusing on mine. "Love the Lord your God with all your heart and all your soul, and all your strength" (Deut. 6:5 NIV).

In spring 2003, God brought me a new friend struggling with addictions. It was through him that I was first introduced to the Gentle Shepherd in Whalley. Together, we attended Alcoholics (AA), Narcotics (NA), and Cocaine (CA) Anonymous meetings throughout the city, where a whole new world opened up. I met men and women struggling with various kinds of addictions—pornography and sex, drugs and alcohol. These were average people like you and me who had somehow become derailed from life. These people were real, open, and honest. They confessed their mistakes and openly admitted their powerlessness over their drugs of choice—not only to themselves but also to God and total strangers. These were courageous people sharing their raw, heartbreaking stories and bravely walking through recovery together.

I came to the realization that there was something familiar about the stories shared in those rooms. I realized I had lived it. Alcohol and drug addiction had been the third partner in my first two marriages. These marriages had failed because of addiction issues with my partners. I spent a brief season with illegal drugs during those relationships, but thankfully when I gave my heart to the Lord, I was spared from slipping into a life of substance abuse.

I wasn't spared completely. Here's a part of my story I never talk about. Remember earlier when I described myself as weak? During my second marriage, I became addicted over a three-year period to a legal drug prescribed to help me cope with the excruciating pain of daily, debilitating migraines, headaches I had suffered with since my early teens. Fiorinal C ½, a sneaky, venomous opiate and barbiturate, almost took me down. It became my poison. It took three weeks of detox, with God and a team of loving medical professionals in a Vancouver chronic pain clinic, to free me from its deadly grip. I was lucky. I got free.

I was called "normie" in those recovery meetings. In other people's eyes, I was normal because I didn't have an addiction you could see. But I felt far from normal. Being honest with myself, I wasn't any different from the others attending these meetings. I understood the grip of addiction. I understood detox. I too had a need to self-medicate, to blot out the deep ache in my soul. The difference was that my real drugs of choice   money and success—were accepted and even encouraged by society. Money and success are as deceptive, destructive, and addictive as any drug out there.

I began the work of my own recovery using the tools of the 12-Step Program, which God used to pull me out of denial and reveal the truth about me. The cover of my "pain box" came off. My Saviour became my sponsor and through hours of prayer and reflection, He revealed the reasons behind my pain, fear of loneliness, and resulting co-dependency. I began the gut-wrenching process of surrender, confession, repentance, and forgiveness.

One morning during this season of recovery, while walking with God along the ocean, deep in thought, out of nowhere I heard, "Father to the fatherless."

Nothing more, just four words. Instantly I knew what they meant. Known only to Him, and hidden from me, I had continued to grieve the loss of my beloved father decades earlier. His death had spun my life out of control and was the root cause of my incessant search for love. My father's death had broken my heart and left me alone and lost with no one to find me. To avoid the suffocating pain, I had never allowed the heartbreak—buried so deep—to surface. Had never seen the connection. Never let it go. All these years, stuck in my loss and grief. Stuck, despite the countless hours of counselling. Trapped, regardless of my daily relentless pursuit to soothe the deep ache in my soul.

God had been preparing my heart through it all, allowing pain to do its work. Only He knew when the time was right. When my heart was ripe for healing—as always—He stood close by. "The LORD is close to the broken-hearted and saves those who are crushed in spirit" (Ps. 34:18 NIV).

In that moment beside the ocean, He held my heart in His Hands. "He heals the broken-hearted and bandages their wounds" (Ps. 147:3 ESV).

He revealed my pain. "The Lord is full of compassion and mercy" (James 5:11 NIV).

He let me release my sorrow. "Praise the LORD, my soul; all my inmost being, praise His holy name ... who redeems your life from the pit and crowns you with love and compassion" (Ps. 103:1, 4 NIV).

The revelation washed over me. My spirit was reborn. My broken heart, yearning for love, finally broke open to accept His. I wasn't alone. I had a Papa. A heavenly Papa! In a nanosecond, the dam of my grief broke. A flood gushed forth. "Weeping may last for a night, but joy comes with the morning" (Ps. 30:5 NLT).

From that second onwards, God began to heal my heart in the deepest way. I felt the *shift* within me.

I walked from the ocean's tide and into the life He had called me to. Smack into a small church in Whalley, in one of the darkest areas of the city. There I found others who were broken-hearted too—the poor and homeless living on the street. "A father to the fatherless, a defender of widows, is God in his holy dwelling. God sets the lonely in families ..." (Ps. 68:5-6 NIV).

In the midst of suffering humanity—after years of searching for love in all the wrong places—I found Jesus, the Lover of my soul.

DISCUSSION QUESTIONS

1. **What is your painkiller?**
   - How do you deal with your pain, loss or loneliness?

2. **What shame and self-blame do you put upon yourself?**

3. **Can your broken heart accept God's love? If not, why not?**
   - Who or what do you turn to, to cope?
   - What would it feel like to turn to God?
   - What would happen if you surrendered and let God show you another way?
   - What would it take to put God first in your life?

Chapter 4

CHRISTMAS DINNER

I N THE YEAR before that *shift*, in that last year of coming to terms with my broken heart, I was also seriously conflicted by my reaction to homeless people. I wanted to be as accepting as Pastors Steen and Lyn Laursen of the Gentle Shepherd Church, who seemed able to look at these broken people and see their goodness—their souls, if you will. But I could not get past the surface of things. I saw filth, and squalor, and addiction.

I did not see myself as a good candidate for street ministry, struggle as I might to do the right thing. I was still questioning God. How could He use me when I was so broken? I felt I was in no state to help others. But God assured me that if I took the first step, He'd do the rest. We'd work through this together.

I would visit the dingy setting of the Gentle Shepherd Church, a decrepit building on the King George Highway in Whalley—at the time an area of the Lower Mainland perhaps even more desperate than Vancouver's infamous Downtown Eastside. On steamy, rainy nights, the rank smell inside was so overwhelming that the doors were kept open. Constant traffic and eighteen-wheelers blasted down the highway. This was the highway that was home to people who, after the service, huddled under blankets for the night in doorways and back alleys, some under trees wrapped in canvas in the local parks.

Seemingly oblivious to the deprivation around them, Pastors Steen and Lyn led a lively service, but I would be thinking: *How in the world have I arrived in such a place as this?* It seemed a lifetime away from my business in Vancouver and the comfortable life I had previously enjoyed. Here I was, in the worst section of the city, in the midst of social outcasts—the poor, drug-addicted, and homeless people—in an area where I would normally have locked my car in fear as I passed through on business. This was foreign territory so unfamiliar that I might as well have been on Mars. I wondered if a third-world mission trip might look like this.

The odour of bleach was overwhelming. So was the rank smell of bodies that had not seen a bath or shower in months. There wasn't a square inch where I felt comfortable enough to sit down without fear of contamination. I was absolutely consumed with fear and acutely aware of how little I had in common with "those" people. I was different. I didn't belong here. I stood at the back of the room—with my back glued to the wall—and watched a scene straight out of a horror movie. People stooped low with decaying teeth and dirty, dishevelled hair, torn, ragged clothing, and filthy hands stood in line waiting for soup, coffee, and a sandwich. I studied each face carefully, expecting to see attitude, but I wasn't given any. They mostly just looked through me.

Through cracked windows, I could see people outside on the sidewalk, "dancing" like puppets controlled by an unseen puppeteer, completely oblivious to the world around them. The street culture calls this "flailing"—the result of using crystal meth. A rancid smell floated by from a huddle of people sucking on clear pipes, inhaling a drug I had never heard of before. Crack. A few pitiful souls were leaning against the wall of the building, "nodding." A puzzling scene—one minute awake and the next moment nodding as if asleep. Heroin. The pavement was peppered with trash, drug debris, and needles used to inject the poison.

Each time I went back to the street church, my heart pounded with fear. I was terrified of "those people," but I was drawn to their devastation and pain. It felt somehow vaguely familiar. I didn't say much to anyone in those early days. I was a stranger in their world and no one knew me. Somehow that brought me comfort. It became a place for me to hide from my own world and my own pain.

Well, as I said: God had assured me that if I took the first step He would do the rest. That *shift* came one Christmas night at a dinner hosted by the Gentle Shepherd.

It was the first time I had travelled to that area by myself; a friend who had promised to join me had backed out at the last minute. It was Christmas. I was alone and feeling sorry for myself. As I entered the Ukrainian Orthodox Church where the meal was being served, I was overwhelmed with the size of the gathering. Families struggling with poverty sat side by side with people from the street, all there to celebrate Christmas. My heart stirred to see this community together. The place was decorated to the nines. A brightly lit Christmas tree stood in one corner, piled high with stockings and surrounded by wrapped presents.

Not knowing what to else do, I slipped into gear and got busy. I grabbed steaming plates of hot turkey, swimming in gravy, and made my way along the rows of brightly coloured paper-clothed tables. The gratitude and joy on the faces I saw were a delight. My heart was captivated.

One gentle soul stood out. He sat by himself in tattered clothes, obviously in a drugged state. Nodding, his nose coming ever closer to the table, finally he passed out face down in a plate of mashed potatoes and gravy. You can imagine the mess. I looked around for someone with more experience to help but no one came to his rescue. All I could think of was how I would feel if this had happened to me. Didn't he deserve respect and dignity?

I stepped forward and gently lifted his head to clean him up. His face was full of open sores, which might have been the reason why others were cautious to run to his aid. I wiped his face with the napkins I carried, carefully tending to his facial sores, and helped him sit up straight in his chair. I returned to the kitchen to collect another plate and I heard the whispered words: "He's the least of these."

I vaguely remembered reading these words somewhere in scripture but I didn't have a clue where to locate them or what they meant. Weeks later, God revealed the full passage: "For I was hungry and you gave me something to eat, I was thirsty and you gave me something to drink,

I was a stranger and you invited me in, I needed clothes and you clothed me, I was sick and you looked after me, I was in prison and you came to visit me . . . Truly I tell you, whatever you did for one of the least of these brothers and sisters of mine, you did for me" (Matt. 25:35-36, 40 NIV).

That cold, crisp Christmas was a turning point in my healing journey. In that moment at that Christmas dinner, I had broken through my resistance. I saw it clearly. All my life, I had walked with pain. That pain had shaped who I was. Now that pain became the common denominator on the street.

"I see you."

There was an understanding—an acceptance—between the street people and me. We understood pain. We all walked in pain. Without a word spoken, we shared a powerful communication. Love followed pain, and the two became unlikely allies and began to work miracles in my life and in the lives of the people God brought across my path.

As I found the courage and the willingness to step forward in obedience, He used me. And He healed me. Through the healing process, He crafted in me a heart of compassion and empathy for those who were hurting.

Gradually, I began to peer out from behind my mask. As I began to connect with people, my problems paled in comparison to theirs. I began to stop feeling sorry for myself. While I was in the presence of those in that shelter, I forgot my own misery. Over the months that followed, people became less scary. They became people. Eventually, they became friends and family.

I was shocked to discover I could be myself with them, that they accepted me just as I was. I didn't have to try to please them to make them like me. I didn't have to pretend I was someone else, the way I had for most of my life. I could be real. I could be the person God had created me to be.

I was free to step into me.

DISCUSSION QUESTIONS

1. **Are you conflicted by your reaction to the 'least of these'?**
   - What are your fears or feelings about people living on the street?
   - Do you ignore, resist or open your heart to them?
   - Do you believe God will do the same for you?
   - Who are the 'least of these' in your community?

2. **How can you bring compassion and empathy for those who are hurting?**
   - What are some ways you are encouraged to do things you wouldn't normally do—how do you respond?

3. **What would it look feel like for you to 'step into yourself'?**
   - In what situations are you free to be yourself? Why? Why not?
   - How could you become more comfortable with yourself?
   - Do you see God in this process?

Chapter 5

GENESIS

NIGHTSHIFT GREW IN concept and in infrastructure out of these first weeks at the Gentle Shepherd when volunteers spent the night at church, watching over the broken lives of street people and assembling the ideas and inspiration for a street ministry for the Whalley homeless and others living in dire, abusive poverty.

"Since its inception in January 2004," our handout information reads, "NightShift has consistently provided assistance to people living in poverty—on the streets and in desperate need of help." What began as a one-hot-meal-a-day program grew into a full-time street ministry that continues over the years to innovate, add services, and change lives.

Because I'm telling the story and I'm telling it from my point of view, that might give the impression that I think I'm responsible for all that happened. But make no mistake—God is responsible for every ounce of NightShift's growth. Many people, including me, played a part in the birthing and upbringing of this organization, but in no way can anybody take credit for NightShift but Him. I'll take responsibility for the mistakes. Only God is responsible for the successes.

The name came about as a response to the long, brutal overnight hours that no one wanted to do. At first, it was just called the *shift*, the tough, dark, exhausting, overnight shift. It evolved to NightShift.

Over time, the name took on a whole new dimension. It signified a *shift*—from darkness to the light of the cross in the lives of those we met. Hardened hearts *shifting*, melting like butter. Personally, it also represented the *shift* in my own life and for many others, the *shift* in the lives of those who were called to serve.

More darkly, NightShift came to represent a *shift* into conflict—the long, dark night of unrelenting opposition and obstruction to our existence. I think of these attacks as spears thrown to stop us. Some spears were thrown in anger, some in cold calculation. We had no idea of the fear, hatred, and organized resistance that would rise against us. You might think hatred is too strong a word, but it's unlikely you and your friends have ever been called "cockroaches who leave their filth behind them."

"Gonna be a long night," the song says.

"NightShift" by the Commodores became our anthem. We sang it together many times—out of tune, but joyously.

Gonna be a long night, it's gonna be all right,
on the nightshift.

At the end of a long day, it's gonna be okay,
on the nightshift.
Oh, you found another home. I know you're not alone,
on the nightshift.
Your love it lifted us higher and higher.
Keep it up and we'll be there at your side,
on the nightshift.
It's gonna be all right,
on the nightshift.

And it wasn't only volunteers who helped create and shape NightShift; it was the street people themselves.

The women on the street particularly impacted me. Women with no hope. The only life they knew was the constant feeding of their addictions, "working" the streets, and committing crime to maintain their drug habit. They were chained to their drug habit, kept prisoner by the enemy of their souls. Unworthy, ashamed, unloved, dirty, and helpless were the tattoos needled into their broken hearts. Most of them, if not all of them, had suffered from severe abuse from early childhood and lived with the consequences every day since. The prospect of a normal life felt unreachable. Unattainable. They appeared hard-core and "street smart"—masters in survival—but underneath the squalor, God showed me women who were kind, loving, and compassionate.

Their pain looked much like mine. It had entered their lives in childhood through the loss of a loved one, abuse, loneliness, rejection, abandonment, or betrayal. I ran from pain after the death of my father and had continued to run in fear for most of my life. When that pain surfaced, it was overwhelming. I was scared of it; I felt suffocated by it; and I would do almost anything to get rid of it. These women also ran from their pain—except they ran to the street, to flee their abusers, to hide, to medicate, to do anything that would kill it. And eventually kill them.

These women and I had other things in common. While we were running from pain, we were also running from the God who loves us. In our decisions to run, to do things by ourselves, we also decided to reject God. We thought much the same: "If God hasn't saved us from the pain of our childhoods, then why would we expect Him to save us from the pain of today?"

A few women stand out. I don't use their real names, only their real stories. They are beautiful souls who have stayed in my heart over the years. I cherish the first women at NightShift. They had much to teach me about life, and I appreciate the lessons.

Shelia

Shelia lived with a lifetime of pain, addiction, and abuse. She had piercing blue eyes and an infectious sense of humour. Her laughter masked her pain and loss. It helped her to cope with a dysfunctional relationship with an abusive man on the street. She wanted desperately to leave him and the street to lead a "normal life." She had a few teeth remaining and her joke was that all she wanted for Christmas was her two front teeth. But what she most desperately wanted, she confided in me in her tears and prayers, was to have her children back. A normal life with children, natural for most women, yet for Shelia, on the streets, addicted, desperate, lost, it felt unattainable.

Wanda

After that first night of keeping watch in the shelter, the next morning I was shaken by the noise of banging on the front door. It became increasingly louder and more threatening.

Wanda, the woman outside hammering on the door, screamed, "Let me in! That blonde woman! I'm going to kill her."

My heart thumped big time as I looked desperately around at the other people in the room for the cause of her anger. I didn't see any other blondes. I realized with a bolt of fear that the threats were aimed at me. I was the blonde woman about to be killed.

Wanda was one tough girl, well known for fighting and causing trouble. Apparently, she had been banned from a nearby shelter and some of the volunteers at the Gentle Shepherd thought she should be banned from our church too. Somehow Wanda blamed me for the decision. I didn't like the idea of banning anyone—I didn't then, and I still don't now—and I opened the door and gave Wanda what she really wanted: to be treated with respect and given a second chance.

Within days, Wanda became a different person. In fact, while I was reviewing past newspaper articles for this book, I came across a picture of us. We were hugging. It's amazing what God's love and kindness can do!

Janice

Janice was a woman struggling with an addiction to heroin. She had a wicked sense of humour, which kept me chuckling and helped us cope with the pain and sadness around us. She broke into a happy dance when she was joyous. I remember her happy dance as she made her way to "work" one night, celebrating what she thought was a miraculous find—a baggie of pot. For her, this was a means for sleep when morning finally arrived. She never slept in the night, particularly not during freezing cold nights in sub-zero temperatures. "I don't fall asleep," she told me. "I'm afraid if I do, I might not wake up." The pot was her undoing. After finding her weeping and doubled over in pain in front of the church, we carried her indoors. She must have fallen asleep. She was absolutely frozen and incapable of moving. It was only after we rubbed her feet, wrapped her in blankets, and warmed her with hot tea that she began to respond and recover. Her sad eyes revealed defeat and pain. Happiness, even stoned-out happiness, was, as always, unattainable. Yet somehow we saw in her eyes profound gratitude—for someone cared about her. Someone finally cared.

That first shelter season, I embraced the reality of one of God's promises to me: "I can do all things through Christ who strengthens me" (Phil. 4:13 NKJV) and I grasped some of the meaning, "… that I may know Him and the power of his resurrection, and the fellowship of his sufferings, being conformed to His death" (Phil. 3:10 NKJV).

As I struggled with the challenge of staying awake night after night, I experienced firsthand the anointing of the Holy Spirit, "and if the Spirit of him who raised Jesus from the dead is living in you, he who raised Christ from the dead will also give life to your mortal bodies through his spirit who lives in you" (Rom. 8:11 NIV).

I worked the nightshift and went home by 8:00 in the morning, only to rise again and return by 6:00 that same night for another shift. I did this for seven nights running, with little sleep. I can attest firsthand that the empowerment of the Holy Spirit is real!

Sheri

One of the women who hugely impacted my heart was struggling with cancer, drug addiction, and AIDS. Sheri was a mess. She mumbled incessantly, which made it very difficult to understand what she was saying. During the night, she screamed in her sleep, disturbing everyone around her. Her groaning felt demonic. No one dared to go anywhere near her! This was scary stuff.

I felt God nudge me to go to her. Here was an opportunity to demonstrate God's power in a huge way. I could hardly move for fear. If I thought I was frightened before, nothing can describe the fear in my heart as I crouched down beside her and placed my hands on her feet. She had no conscious awareness of my presence. In my panic, I had forgotten all I had learned in prayer ministry. Talking about it had been one thing; doing it was quite another. Either I believed Jesus could save or I didn't. Here I was, faced with a real situation, and everything I knew was stripped away. I didn't know what else to do but to whisper the name of Jesus under my breath over and over again. Nothing more, just His name.

Every time I said the name, Sheri's shouting and writhing stopped. When I removed my hands, it began again.

I could feel the Holy Spirit's presence and anointing in a powerful way. I had heard of miracles like this before but had never personally experienced God move through me. Everyone in the room saw God move. No one could deny it. The next morning, Sheri was like a different person. I hardly recognized her. Her countenance was soft, her face radiant. She articulated perfectly and actually held a conversation. She still suffered from her addiction and the sickness that was trying to kill her, but something had shifted in her spirit. We all witnessed this transformation.

This same woman, years later, would become the inspiration for our Care Cottages.

Crissy

Already, by the second night, people began to feel safe in sharing their personal stories of pain, crime, and addiction. Through the long hours of the night, tears, hugs, and prayers were a common sight. We started to connect, bond, and become a family. We were providing something that was not the norm in Whalley back in those days. As we described it, "We were putting a lovin' on people." And everybody felt it.

As families do, we had to establish some basic rules. A few obvious ones like no swearing, weapons, fighting, or doing drugs were put in place. On a regular basis we hammered on the bathroom door, threatening to knock it down if we suspected people to be "using." One woman in particular, whose nickname was Crissy, was loud and threatening. She pushed all the rules to the limit that first night, one of which was about using drugs in the bathroom.

While serving in the kitchen, I overheard some of our overnight guests talking about her being banned from the shelter by one of our team members. I was concerned about what would happen to her if she stayed out in the freezing temperatures. Hours later, I asked one of the street women if she knew where Crissy had ended up. She was found in the snowbank in the parking lot across the street, shivering from the cold. I pulled rank, which caused a hissy fit with the workers who had kicked her out, and asked her friends if they could get her back inside. They carried her through the door, freezing cold and shivering uncontrollably. We had to rub her hands and feet between ours to restore circulation. Finally, wrapped in warm blankets, she settled in for the night.

When she appeared again the next evening, she was a different woman. While still loud and threatening, a softer side was starting to emerge. She asked me for cleaning supplies and though I was dubious about her request, I supplied her with rags and bleach. Crissy marched into the bathroom, which was so dirty and disgusting that I had to plug my nose to enter. It was covered with blood from needle use. Urine and feces were everywhere. I have never seen such a revolting sight or smelled a more repulsive odour in my life. It didn't bother my street friends at all. They were grateful for a bathroom. They were not permitted to use the public facilities at local restaurants or gas stations. The alternative? The bush.

Crissy proceeded to clean it from top to bottom. Using a soiled sheet as a makeshift shower curtain, she hid the ugliness of the ransacked tub. She brought cleanliness and femininity to that hellhole. That spoke buckets to me about her heart, her upbringing, and who she was as a person. This was her way of showing her gratitude for our kindness. We took a liking to each other immediately. From that time on, she watched my back with a vengeance. She had a sense of right and wrong and insisted on respect and order. She barked instructions to everyone on how she thought we should run things. I have to admit, she taught me much about the street culture, drugs, and how to run an emergency shelter.

One night, Crissy was so sick that she was delirious. She refused to go to the hospital for a couple of reasons: one, because it was a well-known fact that drug addicts aren't treated with much respect in admitting; and two, she'd suffer "dope sickness" caused by not injecting heroin.

In the early hours of the morning, I begged her to allow us to take her to the hospital. She refused an ambulance but finally agreed to go if I could take her and stay with her. We carefully deposited her in the back seat of a volunteer's truck and headed for emergency. As expected, the reception was callous. I was shocked at how she was treated but understood that in a busy hospital, staff had to be sensitive and selective in responding to the crises they faced on a regular basis. A dope-sick drug addict, who was abusive in speech and demeanour, didn't elicit an overwhelming amount of tender loving care from intake attendants.

As it turned out, Crissy was admitted just in time. An infection had travelled up her spine; the next stop would have been her heart. She was placed on IV antibiotics in emergency care. We stayed by her side for the rest of the night and for the next three weeks. I fell in love with that girl and saw her potential. I kept telling her how much God loved her and that He had a plan and a purpose for her life, "For I know the plans I have for you," declares the LORD, "plans to prosper you and not to harm you, plans to give you hope and a future" (Jer. 29: 11 NIV).

Crissy attributes the saving of her life to me. I attribute her saved life to answered prayer and the grace of our Lord Jesus Christ. It took five years, with many trips to hospitals and multiple prison visits, to see this woman become clean and sober. She is now reunited with her family and has become part of mine. The woman I first met in our emergency shelter eight years ago has volunteered and worked for the ministry over the years. She now heads up our Extreme Weather Shelter, helping women and men just like her, who struggle with the battle of addictions every day.

And so, it is true: not all dreams of normalcy are unattainable.

DISCUSSION QUESTIONS

1. **Have you ever felt God's spirit or power move through you?**
   - How?
   - Where were you?
   - How did you respond?

2. **Shift doesn't come easy.**
   - Have you had a shift?
   - Describe a time when your hardened heart shifted and softened.
   - What obstacles have been put in your way to moving towards your own shift?
   - How can you take those obstacles down?

3. **Like the women on the street:**
   - What is the one thing you yearn for?
   - What is the second chance you need?
   - Why is happiness unattainable for you?
   - Has the power of prayer ever changed you? How?
   - What happens when you reach out and love others?

Chapter 6

MONEY

———————————————➤

I N THE FIRST days following the snowstorm and the
origins of NightShift, I began wrestling with God—like
Jacob with the angel—about my future.

Would it be commerce or commitment?

Two fears controlled most of my life. Fear of loneliness.
Fear of lack. My mother, widowed at an early age with a
family to feed, watched every cent in order to adequately
provide for our upbringing. It appears I inherited her worry.
I felt the gut-wrenching panic of not having enough money
to survive. How could God be asking me to step away from
my career when I was the one who had provided for myself
year after year? I had no one else to lean on and no means
of support other than what I earned by my own hand. I had
mastered keeping these major fears well hidden, even from
myself, so I didn't have to look at the ugliness of this truth.

I ran into the wrong relationships to deflect my fear of
being alone, but financially I was much more successful.

I relied on me and provided for my own financials needs. I was a capable capitalist who didn't have to depend on anyone else—including God.

Funny, how I could depend on God for other needs in my life. I had witnessed firsthand how He brought me through years of pain, loss, and heartache. Yet when it came to my finances, I trusted myself. Numero uno. I wasn't greedy, I gave to charity—I was a little driven, maybe—but I'd learned to look after myself and it was one thing I was pretty good at doing.

That's really all I was asking of Him. But Jesus had a reason for saying, "It's easier for a camel to pass through the eye of a needle than for a rich man to enter the Kingdom of Heaven" (Mark 10:25 NKJV). God knew my pursuit of money and success had veered me off the path and made me take my eyes off Jesus.

Songwriter Randy Newman penned and sings a cruel, satirical song about such choices. An exaggeration, for sure, but in plain black and white:

> Used to worry about the poor
> But I don't worry anymore
> Used to worry about the black man
> Now I don't worry about the black man
> Used to worry about the starving children of India
> You know what I say about the starving children of India
> I say, "Oh, mama"
> It's money that I love
> It's money that I love
> It's money that I love

The wrestling match began that first week I became preoccupied with the shelter. I was supposed to be preparing to speak to the National Association of Home Builders International Builders' Show in Las Vegas, Nevada. One thousand developers and builders were to hear sales and marketing techniques that would increase their home sales and profits. I was scheduled to be a featured speaker. It was a much sought-after opportunity, a huge leg-up for me, a chance to step into the housing industry in the United States at the highest level. By not attending, I would lose out on one of the greatest opportunities of my career.

By the end of that shelter week, I was faced with a decision. Vegas or "Whalley World." Two worlds, light years away! Wealth versus poverty. I knew in my heart that God didn't want me to go. He had dialled down my passion for business and was replacing it with His compassion for the poor. I prayed for the courage, and days before the event, I called Bill Webb, MIRM (Master in Residential Development), in Amelia Island, Florida. Bill had engaged my services for this convention and he was most gracious and assured me that he could find another presenter to step into my place. I remember telling him that my message to the homebuilders now would be to encourage them to give back to those who couldn't afford to buy a home—not really a message American homebuilders were waiting to hear.

I knew in my heart it would only be a matter of time before I'd be faced with another decision: continue to operate my business or not. Otherwise, where was my income going to come from? In no way was I independently wealthy. Money was tight. My modest savings were tucked away in retirement savings plan investments. Financially, I was in no position to shut the doors of The Connor Group, the sole source of my income and support.

My real estate marketing company had barely survived the housing market's downturn and the economic recession. The financial and housing forecasts predicted the upswing at just the time I needed new business. How could I possibly walk away from everything I had worked so hard to build? I could still be a good daughter to Papa. Didn't God understand that I had a plan to make tons of money and give back to charity?

Well, you know how to make God laugh: tell Him your plans.

Twice before in the last twenty years, I had sensed God nudging me to step away from the business world. It had been my heart's desire since I accepted the Lord in 1986 to attend Bible college to obtain a degree in counselling. However, my head had turned to business, not to things of the Lord. This time the nudge was different. More insistent.

I tried to negotiate for more time. There I was, trying to cut a deal with God! I needed another year, two at the most to take advantage of the rebounding real estate market, delete my recessionary debt, and bank enough money to live on comfortably. That wasn't too much to ask, was it Papa? Then we could talk. After that, I could serve You full time in ministry.

This time, the nudge remained persistent. The time was now. I had a sense that He wasn't going to ask me the fourth time. The thought that God could walk away from me and not nudge again was so distressing that I thought I had no other choice but to obey. What He was asking me looked impossible but with God, nothing is impossible. "Jesus looked at them and said, 'With man this is impossible, but with God all things are possible'" (Matt. 19:26 NIV).

At this point, I truly believed God had called me for ministry. This time I was willing to obey and do whatever He asked, "… for such a time as this" (Est. 4:14 NIV). Over and over again, God reminded me of His promises through His Word, "… I have called you by name; you are mine. When you pass through the waters, I will be with you and when you pass through the rivers, they will not sweep over you. When you walk through the fire, you will not be burned; the flames will not set you ablaze" (Isa. 43:1-2 NIV).

If I trusted God, why was I struggling?

God had yet another challenge. He wanted me to look fear straight in the face and claim God's promises in the area of my finances. He wanted my dependency on Him in every area of my life—especially in provision. What I didn't realize was that He was preparing me to lead a faith ministry that had to depend completely on His faithfulness and provision. He wanted me to experience this faith-walk firsthand in my own personal walk.

I consider myself to be a woman of faith. I know God has given me this gift in full measure. "For it is by grace you have been saved, through faith—and this is not from yourselves, it is the gift of God—not by works, so no man can boast" (Eph. 2:8,9 NIV); "… in accordance with the measure of faith God has given each of you" (Rom. 12:3 NIV); and "… fixing our eyes on Jesus, the pioneer and perfecter of our faith" (Heb. 12:2 NIV).

I knew I didn't have enough faith to depend on Him fully for my finances, so I got on my knees and asked for a bucketful of it so I could say with assurance: "Faith is being sure of what we hope for, and certain of what we do not see" (Heb. 11:1 NIV).

As I stepped away from my full-time career into the unknown, He began to move and bless me. Almost immediately, I received a call from a former client, who kindly offered me a part-time paid marketing contract to aid in my financial support. I gratefully accepted the position, a tentmaking opportunity like Paul's. "… He was a tentmaker as they were, he stayed and worked with them"(Acts 18: 3 NIV). It provided me with a little income and the necessary time to deal with the rapidly growing demands of the ministry. However, the work didn't pay nearly enough to meet my hefty financial obligations. When I stepped away from my company, I had taken the debt with me. Now I was depleting my saving account to supplement my monthly income.

By 2005, the ministry had grown significantly, as had the demands for my time. NightShift was competing with my marketing contract, which was quickly moving into a lucrative but full-time commitment. This created much stress as I tried to juggle different responsibilities. It was not fair to my client, the ministry, or me. I was faced with another dilemma. Again, I had a choice. Commit more time to my contract, less time to the ministry. Or commit more time to the ministry and walk away from my income. Here was another temptation, asking me to rely on my own means. The contract work, however beneficial to me at the time, was just another distraction. It held me back from where God was leading me. I confess I was tempted to step back into business more than once, particularly when the opposition to NightShift rose like an invading army. The spears were coming at me and I wanted to retreat for cover.

I made the choice. I took the leap. A leap of faith into full-time ministry—fully dependent on God for provision. My small nest egg had dwindled. I had used all of it, down to the last penny, to support the ministry and myself. I remember the month when I transferred the last dollar from my retirement savings plan account. By that time I had realized that God wanted it all. It belongs to Him anyway, doesn't it? From that month forward and to this day, I walk in faith, trusting God to pay the rent, put food on the table, and put gas in my car. Of course, that same faith and trust applies to NightShift.

The Bible says, "If anyone has material possessions and sees his brother in need but has not pity on him, how can the love of God be in him … let us not love with words or tongue but with actions and in truth" (1 John 3:17-18 NIV).

I took that scripture to heart and did what God asked me to do: give it all. He may not ask you to do the same thing, but I know for sure that's what He asked of me. Why? Because it was such a hard thing for me to do! He knew a huge chunk of my heart was attached to the power of money. He was wrestling it back to where it belonged—in His hands.

I can't honestly say I didn't have moments of intense panic, wondering where the next dollar would come from.

God, in His wisdom and perfect timing, used this season to develop and grow my faith. I can truly say, He always provided for my needs. Rarely early, mind you, but always on time. I never suffered lack. For those of you who walk the faith-walk every day, you know exactly what I mean. I see you smiling and nodding now.

His provisions came in the strangest ways—right down to the smallest detail. Here's one of my favourite stories.

I have a passion for fresh flowers and as a treat I often buy flowers for myself to brighten my day. Money was sparse during those times, and while picking up a few groceries one day, I grabbed a bouquet of flowers before I realized that I probably didn't have enough money to pay for them and my groceries too. I reluctantly put the flowers back. Later that day, I received a telephone call from a stranger—a total, absolute stranger—telling me that he had something to give me.

I had never spoken to this person before and was very uneasy about continuing the conversation further. When I pressed for more information, he said, "It's a surprise." Normally, I would have ignored the call, but something told me it was okay to meet this man at a local Starbucks. It was a public place and that gave me some comfort and safety.

I arrived early and before long I saw a man coming across the parking lot with the largest, most beautiful bouquet of flowers I'd ever seen. They were pure white flowers with various shades of green foliage. Gorgeous. My absolute favourite.

This was a big guy and the flowers cascaded over his arms. He walked through the door and made a beeline straight to my table. In astonishment, I watched him, as if in slow motion, drop the flowers into my arms. I was speechless and so were the people around me watching this unfold. Who was this man? I stumbled out a "Thank you!" to which he replied, "Don't thank me, thank God. He asked me to do this." I half-seriously, half-jokingly asked him if he was an angel, and with a smile and wink, he walked out the door. I haven't seen him since.

I will not forget this for the rest of my life. It felt like God had stooped down from His throne of grace and planted a huge kiss smack on my cheek! Not only was I absolutely delighted—tingles all the way down to the tip of my toes delighted—but also acutely aware that this was God's way of showing me not to worry. He had things covered down to the smallest detail. Ever since that day, when I slide into worry or panic about not having enough to meet the ministry's needs, I hear His soft whisper, "Remember?" And remember I do!

I can almost smell the flowers!

DISCUSSION QUESTIONS

1. **Do you believe in the words of Jesus?**
   - Yes, why?
   - No, why not?

2. **What fears control your life?**
   - Are you facing your fears? How?
   - What bargains are you making with God? How is this working out?
   - Where does God fit in?

3. **Do you trust that God will provide?**
   - When has God provided in an unexpected way?
   - If I trust God, why am I struggling?

4. **What impossible situations are you facing?**
   - How can you serve others in the midst of your situation?
   - Are you prepared to receive God's favour and blessings?

Chapter 7

BUSTED

WEEKS AFTER THE snowstorm that threatened the lives of the homeless on the Lower Mainland of British Columbia, our ministry at the Gentle Shepherd Foursquare Church in Whalley was still operating, providing an overnight place of safety, a hot meal, prayer, and respite for the weary souls living on the streets.

Then, like the pop of a flashbulb, we were news.

"From Real Estate To Real Compassion," the headline read on the front page of *The Surrey Leader*. "Real Estate Magnate Closes Her Business To Work Full-time With The Homeless."

Staff reporter Kevin Diakiw had sniffed out the story and called me for an interview. I was uncomfortable about the idea. My history had taught me to be cautious with reporters. I'd worked with them in the past, usually promoting my real estate clients' charity campaigns—like Every Woman's Dream Home for breast cancer research—and I knew how careful you had to be with reporters if you wanted them to write the story you wanted them to write. (It's why campaign managers always insist their political candidates "stay on message.") I did not want this story to be about me and I invited Pastor Steen and one other person to join us. But my strategy didn't work.

Diakiw is a skilled reporter, who was obviously working on an agenda of his own. Throughout the interview, he asked probing questions about my background and my place in the story. I thought I just as skilfully had deflected them to my two companions—but after the first half dozen or so questions, I had a sinking feeling. He kept pursuing me in the interview. It was my first media interview about the ministry and I guess I was outmanoeuvred. Afterwards, I quietly reminded him that the shelter wasn't about me. It was about God and the people without homes. He looked me straight in the eye and said very seriously, "You're the story."

One quote from me hit the nail on the head: "The pay isn't great, but the rewards are invaluable!" Diakiw's article set off a wave of support and a tsunami of protest. Other publications followed—some against our ministry, the majority for us.

Later that year, in *BCBusiness*, the province's leading business news magazine, journalist Myles Murchison described his night at the Gentle Shepherd:

Outside, through the open door, the semis blast down King George Highway. Inside, we sing with a band of hard-thumping God rockers—Revive me! Reviiiiiive me!—when, just like a miracle, loaves of bread appear in the doorway and are carried over the heads of the 50 or so homeless souls to the kitchen where the aroma of a tall tureen of bubbling beef stew has managed to overcome the stink of damp clothing. In the kitchen, coaxing another night from the three working elements on the old electric stove, is the business woman who has indeed revived this place—thank you, Jesus—a woman who for years fought against this call, who resisted what she says is the word of God, who lived in another world of upscale condos that had that new-home smell, where commission deals were cut with eager buyers on the backs of brochures, where she and her former husband glamorously floated away their lives on a houseboat. She was a hard-ass real estate sales and marketing consultant who could out-talk, out-hustle and out-work the best of them.

But you can only resist God's word for so long—ask Moses, ask Paul … and ask MaryAnne Connor.

She's here in the kitchen, distributing the loaves and dishing out the beef stew in Styrene cups with plastic spoons, MaryAnne Connor who has brought her entrepreneurial intuition and the black arts of a sales-wise condo promoter to rescue a street mission for the homeless, MaryAnne Connor who believes, whether we know it or not, we are all in the service of God—Can I hear "Amen"? (*BCBusiness*, October 2004)

Stories like these put us on the map, but in the process, caused much too much controversy. We were now on the radar screen. And, thanks to these stories, I was the target.

It didn't take long for accusations to follow. The rumour was that I was "trying to make a buck" by coming to Whalley. Murchison, who is also an old friend and colleague from my days in the real estate industry, came to my defence.

> Connor does naturally what one is trained to do in business leadership seminars: she models the desired behaviour. At the mission she's the approachable one most people there know as "Mac" ... she puts in the 12-hour overnights, the day-to-day meetings with civic and business people, the personal one-on-one contact. But there's something more: Connor has genuine mainstream charisma. She appears to be what she believes she is: guided. "God did that," she tells me when something positive happens. She also has what spiritual leaders need to succeed: the ability to attract cohorts ... Doing good works for profile and good PR, that's easy for all of us media-cynical people to understand, but to do something simply because Jesus would? Where's the profit? What's the motivation? (*BCBusiness*, October 2004)

What most people couldn't understand—or were mighty suspicious about—was that my motivation was personal. I believed with all my heart that this was what God had called me to do. He had rescued me. He had saved me from the pit. He had accomplished a miraculous work in my heart. He had healed, restored, and redeemed my life. In deep gratitude, I wanted to give it all back to Him. To use me as He wills. To help others who needed rescuing. How could I not? My personal and business goals had changed dramatically. My personal mission statement reads, "To live a surrendered, crucified life in Christ, walking in the power of His resurrection, imitating Him in humility, purity, servanthood, holiness, righteousness, and godliness."

I know it makes some people uneasy to hear it, but my profit is in heaven. My motivation is God.

Whatever my motivation, however, the story had broken. I had been naive not to understand what a public issue homelessness was, and that it was about to blow back on our ministry with unmasked hostility and organized resistance.

"We have some disturbing news to share," I wrote our supporters in April 2004. "The City of Surrey has made a decision to shut down our overnight program."

The reason for the closure was technically a bylaw infraction. Even though it's a bona fide church, apparently the Gentle Shepherd was not zoned for an overnight shelter. I received a call from a City of Surrey bylaw officer, instructing me to shut down the overnight operation of the shelter by April 1, 2004. We were given less than twenty-four hours' notice.

We complied but we didn't quit. We continued to operate from nine to midnight on Friday and Saturday nights while we petitioned for support to continue services.

That same month, Andrew Holota, editor of *The Surrey Leader*, wrote:

> The hungry are left to search for an ever-changing roster
> of resources as the caring people who operate them

scramble for new locations. There is a reason for this. Part is the tacit belief that the poor somehow deserve to be derelict—because they abuse drugs, or don't try hard enough, or any of the multitudes of reasons the more affluent frequently use to dismiss the real needs of the less fortunate. This is NIMBYism (not in my backyard) that makes it difficult for helping organizations to take root, or encounter public opposition when they do. The other part is simply a lack of organization. For those who are living on the street, or very near to it, the issue is a simple one. Folks are hungry. They need consistent, stable assistance, from the basics to long-term strategies. There are people out there who are willing to help. Now, let's get organized and make it happen.

We had been doing exactly what Holota advised. We were attempting to get organized, gathering church and community support, establishing a board, and registering as a not-for-profit charity organization. But opposition to our continued existence was pervasive. It seemed that for every forest fire I put out, more bush fires popped up. For every two steps forward, we were pushed back ten. Every time we advanced, we faced another spear aimed straight at us.

By May 2004, the City of Surrey was organized against us, and—as I was soon to discover—so was the official arm of the business community. I didn't have a lot of street smarts in those days; I assumed the business community would see the plight of the poor and willingly work together with the faith community to help bring about positive solutions. I know it sounds idealistic—work together to help those on our streets and to make a better community—but that was my heart.

What it required was someone to take on the burden at street level, and we were willing.

I learned that a Whalley Enhancement Strategy plan was in the works. I thought we should get involved and become part of the solution. After all, people living on the street are part of the community, aren't they? So, being proactive, I initiated a meeting with the Whalley Business Improvement Association (WBIA) on May 5, 2004.

What I didn't know was that we were walking straight into spears.

My friend Myles Murchison was researching his story for *BCBusiness* at the time and he came to the WBIA meeting with me. We could feel the wall of anger as we walked through the door that day.

Inside the boardroom, I was escorted to a seat at the head of the table. The president sat to my right, with about nine other people scattered along either side. There was some nervous conversation to start. When they learned that Murchison was a journalist from *BCBusiness*, tensions erupted. People were very uncomfortable with that. Somehow I convinced them to let him stay. Then, with my best presentation skills, I launched into our vision of NightShift working arm-in-arm with business. There wasn't a smile in the room.

When I was finished, they wanted to know why I was doing this. I tried to explain. The answer was so obvious.

Murchison told me later that I answered the way Jesus might.

"'Do unto others as you would have them do unto you?' They simply couldn't buy into the notion," he said. "It was as if you were talking to the Pharisees. You might as well have been speaking in Aramaic."

The questions started flying. This was not going to be a friendly discussion. This was turning into an out-and-out interrogation. Who were these people? I realized too late I hadn't done my homework.

The major concern was that NightShift was attracting homeless people into the area. "Like a magnet," they said. My inside voice said, "I didn't know we had that kind of power. Weren't these people here before we arrived? Doesn't the SkyTrain service stop in Whalley?" But I was so surprised by their vehemence—they were so entirely and, in some cases, bitterly opposed to our belief and goals—that I couldn't find the right arguments to sway them to our view. I should say, God's view.

I'd certainly had better meetings.

In his story for *BCBusiness*, Murchison wrote, "The last question comes from Pete Nichols, president of the WBIA, and a stand-up-and-be-counted guy: 'What will you do if the community doesn't want you there?' Connor, a stand-up-and-be-counted personality herself, says: 'We'll do it anyway.'"

On my behalf—at the risk of sounding defensive—I thought Pete Nichols' question meant what would we do if the WBIA didn't support us. My answer, that we'd do it anyway, meant that we'd find business and financial assistance some other way. My response was not intended to be arrogant or defiant. I would never do that. It was a

very matter-of-fact proposition to me. We certainly weren't
going to quit. We would simply go back the next day and
open the doors just like we had been doing for months. I
didn't know we needed their permission. Did we? I'd gone
to that meeting as a good neighbour to introduce NightShift
and to hopefully receive their blessing and support.

Remember: I did say I was naive.

Murchison's take on the meeting was that the WBIA saw
Whalley in a rather nostalgic and unrealistic way. Myles had
worked at CKNW in New Westminster in the 1960s and
he never remembered crossing the Pattullo Bridge into an
idyllic, rural paradise and driving into a pristine little village.
However, speaking about the WBIA, he wrote in his story,
"These people don't see Whalley as another Downtown
Eastside. They see Whalley as a once homey neighborhood
changed by SkyTrain, derelict houses and an influx of drug
dealers and pimps who prey on the poor and displaced."

In his subsequent interview with Nichols, Murchison
quotes the then-WBIA president as saying about NightShift,
"We don't need a defiant group that doesn't care what goes
on in this neighbourhood but says, 'Hey businesses, you
have the responsibility of financing us' and that's what
we're getting."

The fight was on.

DISCUSSION QUESTIONS

1. Do you believe you are in the service of God?

2. What does the Bible say about godly character?

3. What attributes should someone who believes in God aspire to?
   - How will this be accomplished in your life?

Chapter 8

HOMELESS

IN JUNE, a month after my meeting with the WBIA, the Gentle Shepherd's landlord presented NightShift with a three-month eviction notice effective August 31, 2004, citing he had obtained a more suitable tenant to occupy the space.

I was confused.

A week previously, I had met with the landlord, who assured me we could stay for as long as we wanted. On reflection, I think the eviction came about because of an issue between the landlord, the city, and the Royal Canadian Mounted Police (RCMP), who served as the city's regular police force. Earlier, the city had applied pressure on our landlord to evict people who were sleeping in the back of the old Pinky's Laundromat located next to the Gentle Shepherd. We knew that because the evicted were street friends of our ministry. *The Surrey Leader* newspaper reported our landlord as saying, "The city was growing weary of the people staying at the ministry." To protect himself from receiving a city fine, he decided to evict us despite having given me his word.

Interesting to note, after our reluctant departure, the church sat empty for years. So much for a more suitable tenant.

Bylaw officials contended they had only directed the landlord to clean up the former laundromat. One bylaw officer said, "I guess he decided to revamp the ministry too." It sure looked suspicious. It looked as if someone or some group was very determined to push us out of the city.

This letter, written from the heart of a woman living on the street, is in response to our eviction notice. She wrote it to the Surrey Mayor and Council.

First you closed our NightShift program when they opened overnight giving us a safe, warm place to sleep. Now you want to close the church down completely. But you forget one thing. The love God gives can't be shut down. The church has helped many change their lives by giving us love, respect, encouragement and direction which each of us needs. Some of us homeless aren't ready to take the step into recovery or the job market. We need first to learn self-respect and self-esteem and to know that somebody cares. Some of us are scared, some just need encouragement and others need to be asked not ordered. NightShift has helped many find that direction in life—love, trust and encouragement and the feeling of being trusted without any type of judgment or discrimination. This enables us to gain enough trust in them to tell them about our problems and our barriers that are stopping us from getting off the street. They have earned our respect for their sincerity, hope and encouragement that they have shown us.

NightShift has given us what you have taken away. They know all our names and greet us with a handshake, smile or gentle touch. They feed us healthy foods, and show us sincere love that comes from their heart. They shed tears of joy and sadness, give advice, take time to listen and help us understand the life we could be living and how to succeed in finding it.

I have a proposition to make to you. I think instead of making decisions based on stereotype opinions, statistics or someone who has never been faced with the challenges of being homeless that you visit our church and see for yourself. If you have the courage or the time to make a surprise visit before this decision is finalized, join us at NightShift in God's house on a Saturday night between 9 pm and midnight, I bet the last penny in my pocket that you would actually see a different picture than that which has been painted for you. You would enjoy yourself. We find our problems disappear and the discouragement, sadness, confusion and decisions on where to find a safe place to sleep that night all lift from your shoulders when we are in this church. You will find laughter, jokes, and conversation that you don't feel or see on the streets.

As a member of the city, I feel you should visit NightShift before a decision is made. You have power but never forget where you originated. God above and none of us would be here without him. The more we pray together the stronger we become. The more God will see that we want this church to stay open. The power of our love for NightShift and the Gentle Shepherd will create an army that no human in this world could fight. You now know our views. Please put a face to the homeless. We are not invisible.

If you don't choose to visit—could a couple of us come and state our views to you with Mac? Whatever decision you make we know that we will have to accept, but not even the city no matter what they take from us can take away our memories and love we found from NightShift and this church.

In God's eyes everyone is equal—we are all his children. So we let this decision rest in God's hands.

Yours truly, Anonymous

Some months later, reporter Kevin Diakiw quoted me as saying the city had to take a more comprehensive look at cleaning up Whalley, "Coming from a business background, I'm totally sympathetic and understand their concern to clean up the city. Our stand on this initiative is that while they're making the effort to clean up Surrey's streets, they need to include cleaning up the street people as well, inside and out" (*The Surrey Leader*, December 2004).

In August 2004, NightShift obtained legal status as a registered not-for-profit charitable society. We assembled a NightShift board under my leadership. We were friends who had served faithfully and who had hearts for recovery and the broken. We had our challenges; we had lots coming at us.

Oddly, one of the challenges was our advisory consultant, who was provided to us by the local ministerial association to help us get organized. For almost two years he guided us, and ironically, he seemed to stir the pot with more conflict than he resolved. His heart was in the right place; I just don't think he understood ragamuffins. I affectionately referred to us as the ragamuffins in reference to Brennan Manning's *Ragamuffin Gospel—Good News for the Bedraggled, Beat-up and Burnt-out*.

"There they are. There we are," Manning wrote, "the multitude who so wanted to be faithful, who at times got defeated, soiled by life, and bested by trials, wearing the bloodied garments of life's tribulations, but through it all clung to faith."

We pounded the pavement looking for another space; we were keenly aware that winter was rapidly approaching. Several potential properties were identified, but once the owners discovered we were serving the homeless community, negotiations quickly shut down. August 31 was a sad day. We packed up our meagre belongings and trucked the contents off to a nearby storage locker. The front door was locked for the last time. I can't describe the devastation that swept over me. Looking through the windows, the same cracked windows that I had peered through months before, all I saw was an empty space. A space as empty as my heart. Memories washed over me as I remembered the countless stories and all the people I had come to know and love.

The bullies had won. Questions swirled around my brain. What had happened? I had walked away from everything to serve God. How could I have been so mistaken? Now what? The broken hearts of my street friends standing with me on the sidewalk broke mine. Defeated, with nowhere to go, we left on our separate paths.

On the first day of September 2004, I awoke instantly with the thought, *We're homeless!*

Just like our street friends, we had no roof over our heads. As I lay there thinking, I felt God speak to my spirit, "Do it anyway."

"What?"

"Do it anyway."

"Do what anyway?"

Then it hit me. He didn't have to say it again. God didn't want us to give up. I shot out of bed and hit the floor running. I was going to Whalley even if I had to make sandwiches myself and serve them out of the trunk of my car.

What had been troubling me was this: we had been with our friends every night for the last eight months. Hearts had softened. Hearts had bonded. People were loved. And loving in return. How could we leave just because we didn't have four walls and a roof over our heads? What did that say? Talk about fair-weather friends! We couldn't abandon them like everyone else had in their lives. I knew with certainty that this was exactly what Papa wanted. Within hours I had gathered a team. Things started to roll. One of my former homebuilder clients and his family offered to cook a big pot of chili. Bible Fellowship Foursquare Church supplied a folding table. Like the legs on that table, everything snapped into place.

We gathered outside the old church location, not sure where or how we were going to serve. Around the corner was Bentley Field, so we headed for it and found a spot to set up. In no time we were ready. People started to appear. One by one, they came. Just like the night of the snowstorm. Oh, what a night!

Glorious.

I stood quietly as we held hands, gathered for our closing prayer circle under the stars, the Holy Spirit hovering over us. The first night of many.

God had said, "Don't box me in."

We were doing exactly what He had intended for this ministry. Homeless ourselves, we were still reaching out. Outreach. Our DNA. Yes, He wanted us to step even further out of our comfort zones and into another world. Embrace where they were. Join their "hood". Our decision to remain in Whalley, in spite of the loss of our building, spoke buckets to our friends. We weren't going to leave. We were there for them. They could trust us. We earned their respect that night.

We came out the next night, and the next, and the next. We kept on going. In darkness or sunlight. Rain or shine. Sleet or hail. Snowstorms. Windstorms. Freezing temperatures. Searing heat. In a field. Under makeshift tarps.

"Don't box me in."

No one knew we were there. That is, until another newspaper article written by Kevin Diakiw appeared in *The Surrey Leader* on September 17, 2004. The headline read, "The hunger doesn't stop—a group evicted from King George building now feeding people on the street."

Stuff hit the fan.

DISCUSSION QUESTIONS

1. **How have you demonstrated love, respect and encouragement to another?**
   - How do you think this has impacted their self-esteem and self-respect?
   - How does your presence encourage others?
   - Do you need love, respect and encouragement? If so, where might you find it? How can you ask for it?

2. **Are you committed to helping others in your community?**
   - Are you, too, prepared to step beyond your comfort zone and enter another world?
   - Are you willing to meet people where they are?
   - Are you prepared to go further?
   - Are you prepared to be challenged?

3. **When have you felt homeless or abandoned?**
   - How did you respond?

Chapter 9

MARY'S HEART

KEVIN DIAKIW'S STORY quoted critics saying we shouldn't be feeding people outside where sanitary conditions couldn't be ensured. He reported that we were also in violation of the city's bylaws, which required appropriate zoning for this type of activity. (We seemed always to be in violation of city bylaws.)

The negative press threatened our continued feeding of the poor and homeless and ignited further outrage and attack on NightShift, spears thrown mostly by people who saw our mission as enabling homelessness and by those who were determined to end our existence.

But the controversy also brought out our supporters. Judy Villeneuve, co-chair of the Surrey Homeless Task Force and a city councillor, said of me, "She's someone who will do what she thinks is right and take it as far as she can to keep people from going hungry. And I admire her for that."

Councillor Villeneuve said she'd rather see the hungry fed by NightShift than scraping food from dumpsters.

The publicity also attracted new volunteers. There was a handful, a core team of faithful volunteers, who were involved from the very beginning. They had the passion and tenacity. Now a groundswell of support started to emerge. The negative publicity had turned the tide. New people started to arrive at our Bentley Field location, extending their hands and hearts to serve. The word was out. Many of these same volunteers remain in faithful service today.

During the first few months, I sensed God saying, "It's bigger than one church." At first I didn't have a clue what He was referring to, but as I looked around me—at the people He was gathering to the street—it slowly dawned on me.

One by one they came. Bigger than one church, they came from different denominations. It didn't matter what church we attended as individuals or what denomination we called our own. What mattered was this: His people were standing shoulder-to-shoulder, serving others with the love of Jesus Christ. He had called them to the street, not me. God was calling His church—in unity, in community—to love and serve in this little organic, grassroots street ministry.

It takes more than one organization, ministry, or church to help those struggling with life's challenges and addictions. As Leonardo Boff, the Brazilian theologian and human rights activist wrote,

What is church? Grassroots Church? Genuine Church? Born at the heart of God's People. A ministry of community coordination, caring for the sick, looking after the poor and homeless, all done with a deep spirit of communion, with a sense of joint responsibility and an awareness of building and living actual church, the ongoing birth and creation of the church: the Holy Spirit.

The power of One.
One God.
One Church.
By the end of September, our volunteer numbers had increased. Every night we had three or four different denominations serving together, feeding the hungry, praying under the stars—it was joyous.

But rain and snow were just around the corner. People were becoming anxious. We still didn't have a roof. It wasn't looking good. We were serving out of the trunks of our cars and the back of trucks. The pressure was on. Some volunteers were becoming discouraged.

Then came a miracle.

One day in November, a volunteer donated a used one-ton cube truck. No, it was more than a truck; it was truly a miracle. We moved our things from our cars to the inside of the vehicle and spread a tarp awning to allow volunteers to serve under all weather. A makeshift counter, quickly assembled, provided a space to prepare peanut-butter-and-jelly sandwiches. Rough wooden shelves were piled high with the blankets, coats, jeans, and various sundries that we had started to collect. A number of churches stepped up to cook hot soup. Other dishes were prepared in the homes of dedicated people in the community with generous hearts just wanting to help in some way. Faithful hands delivered steaming meals. We provided hot food and comfort, dry goods and blessings to the "least of us." All the while, an old rugged cross, crafted by one of our volunteers, stood silently in the shadows, proclaiming that the territory belonged to Jesus.

We were rolling. All was well with my soul. Little did I know that NightShift was about to be battered from all sides, like a ship on an angry ocean. Think of the Prayer of the Breton Fishermen: "O, God Thy sea is so great and my boat is so small." Thankfully, God had prepared me for the storm by exposing the bitterness in my heart. Releasing me from my heart's anger, God gave me a powerful means to defeat the storm, a sort of personal GPS that I would need to guide me through the conflicts in the coming months.

God's lesson began in the first weeks at the Gentle Shepherd, before we received notice from the City of Surrey to shut the shelter down.

Night after night, a trickle of volunteers showed up to help but eventually over time they tended to leave for the comfort of their own beds. I remained with another worker every night doing the overnight shift. As exhaustion began to take its toll, we were desperate for people to join the movement.

I asked God for more hands and feet but soon realized that volunteers, servants, and donors weren't created equal. Over time, I learned that people came to the ministry with different issues and baggage. Not everyone has a pure heart to serve. Some came with motives and agendas very different from the ministry's, with an attitude of doing us a favour by giving of their time or money and service. A spirit of control, entitlement, and self-righteousness often attaches itself to this type of service. It pushes back when corrected or directed.

Sometimes, in gathering hands and feet, we trip over each other. Friction. Nevertheless, our mission is to love people unconditionally. Everyone was welcome to help. And we loved them all without expectations.

To overcome this friction, I began to ask God to gather people with Aaron's heart. Aaron, as you remember from the Bible, was the older brother of Moses, an eloquent speaker and supporter of his brother. Then, with some further study, I realized that I might be asking for the wrong people. Through the book of Exodus, God showed me that Aaron was somewhat fickle in his service to Moses. He quickly turned from Moses' leadership when Moses took too long with God up on the mountain. In fact, he fashioned a golden calf to worship and lied about it when confronted by Moses upon his return. God began to show me an alternative to Aaron. Joshua.

Joshua was a servant who faithfully followed Moses' leadership and often remained behind to continue worshipping God long after Moses had left the tent. I learned the hard way that it wasn't enough to gather hands and feet without leadership. That often resulted in people bumping into each other, causing major friction and disunity. I needed Joshuas. So I began to look around for Joshua hearts.

During this challenging time, I did a lot of reading. One book was titled *Night Shift,* written by David Shive. (Interesting title, don't you think?) It was particularly revealing. Reading Shive's book, I concluded that serving on the shelter's night shift was not a foreign concept for me—I'd been living in the dark for a very long time. Metaphorically, I had been serving on night-shift duty for most of my life.

One of the key areas that became clear as I read Shive's book was that I had unresolved anger and resentment towards God and countless others. Unresolved hurt and anger had taken a bitter root in my soul. God wanted to cleanse me of this poison. He desired a *shift* from bitterness to sweetness—a work that He promised to do in my heart if I could trust Him and surrender to His will.

The devil had pounced on my anger that rose from the hurts and wounds suffered from a lifetime of failed expectations and dreams. I blamed God. I was angry with Him for all the grief and loss in my life. Meanwhile at NightShift, accusations were flying at me from every direction, even from some other believers. I felt spears hitting my back. I didn't have the skills or the know-how to deal with them. Instead, I tucked them away in my heart and stewed.

Now it was time to let go. It was time to confess, repent, and forgive. It was time to heal.

In prayer one day, I asked God how He saw me. He replied with one word, "Mary."

Mary caught my attention.

My street friends know me by Mac, others by MaryAnne. My first name is Mary but no one ever calls me by that name. Only my family knew that Mary was my given name. So I asked Him what He meant by it. He answered, "You have a Mary's heart."

I went digging into His Word in search of the meaning. What I found caused a deep transformation. Mary means

Marah—bitter. The discovery that this name meant bitter made me wonder why God saw and called me by that name. The name confirmed what I secretly thought of myself. I was an angry, bitter woman. The disclosure did not bring me comfort. I was ashamed to be so clearly identified by name.

My continued search led me to Exodus 15:22-26 to the waters of Marah where Moses led Israel from the Red Sea into the desert of Shur. After three days without finding water, they came to Marah and couldn't drink its water because it was so bitter. After Moses cried out to God, the Lord showed him a piece of wood that Moses threw into the water, thus turning its bitterness sweet and making it fit to drink. A strange thing for God to do, but then again anything is possible with God.

I was confused. What did bitter water and a piece of wood have to do with my life? So I asked God for further clarification. He revealed to me what the piece of wood that Moses threw into the water represented. For my heart, it represented the wood of the cross—the old wooden, rugged cross on which Jesus was crucified. Only Jesus' death could conquer the bitterness held in my heart, as I surrendered to His love.

God then began to show me the sweetness of the women named Mary in the Bible. Each one was an ordinary woman. Some fallen, all changed, and all chosen by God to do His work. I'm not including myself in this holy lineup of Marys; I'm only acknowledging the qualities these women modeled.

I saw that God did His deep work in their hearts, just as He did with me. Only Jesus could heal me of the bitter state of my heart and bring forth the sweetness God desired for my life. That such sweetness was attainable for my life was a miracle I was sure even He couldn't achieve—easily "up there" with turning sweet the bitter waters of Marah. But God promised that He would make me sweet. "Amazing Grace, how *sweet* the sound!" Not only is He achieving this in my heart, but He has also shown me how the hearts of the Marys in the Bible represent His heart and must represent the heart of NightShift as we fold new volunteers and servants into His service.

He also taught me important lessons about the difference between a Mary and a Martha heart and to be mindful of being distracted by busyness and not taking the time to sit at His feet.

> As Jesus and his disciples were on their way, He came to a village where a woman named Martha opened her home to Him. She had a sister called Mary, who sat at the Lord's feet listening to what He said. But Martha was distracted by all the preparations that had to be made. She came to Him and asked, "Lord, don't you care that my sister has left me to do the work by myself? Tell her to help me!"
>
> "Martha, Martha," the Lord answered, "you are worried and upset about many things, but few things are needed—or indeed only one. Mary has chosen what is better, and it will not be taken away from her."
>
> —Luke 10:38-42 NIV

So I started asking God for people with Joshua and Mary hearts. People who were heads over heels in love with Jesus and willing to do anything He asked them to do. Anything, even if it meant cleaning toilets. So now, when interviewing people for ministry service, we'll often ask a tongue-in-cheek question, "Will you clean toilets?" Peoples' reactions reveal where their hearts are. I love it that Papa looks at our hearts.

God spoke to me about my ungodly response to some major spear-throwing taking place at the time. Thankfully, He gave me a fast-track lesson in godly conflict resolution skills. Samuel 1 and 2 and *The Tale of Three Kings* by Gene Edwards opened mind-heart-boggling truths. More times than I care to remember, I was before God, at the feet of Jesus, pleading with Him to restore my heart when I recognized again the anger and bitterness I thought I had under control had crept back in.

I was led to stories about David, who had faced severe challenges with Saul and Absalom. He suffered at the angry hands of King Saul, who tried to kill him several times, and because of a disrespectful, rebellious son who tried to usurp his authority and throne. God showed how He wanted me to react to my authorities—in both the church and city—some of whom were abusing their power. God asked me to respond with the opposite spirit, just like David did when he refused to throw spears back at Saul. Instead, David demonstrated a spirit of love and humility. God used David's reaction to Absalom's rebellion to teach me another valuable lesson. When confronted by conflict, or when someone disrespects or challenges my authority (it happens to all of us from time to time), I must always, always respond by speaking the truth in love.

Love, truth, and humility have become powerful weapons in fighting the schemes of the enemy.

Therefore put on the full armour of God, so that when the day of evil comes, you may be able to stand your ground, and after you have done everything, to stand. Stand firm then, with the belt of truth buckled around your waist, with the breastplate of righteousness in place, and with your feet fitted with the readiness that comes from the gospel of peace. In addition to all this, take up the shield of faith, with which you can extinguish all the flaming arrows of the evil one. Take the helmet of salvation and the sword of the Spirit, which is the word of God. And pray in the Spirit on all occasions with all kinds of prayers and requests.

—Ephesians 6:13-18 NIV

However, this is easier said than done! This is not my natural inclination. In my former life, I would have taken things into my own hands. Putting up my dukes, I was always ready to fight. So God had a lot of work to do in me and, believe me, I'm still a work in progress. He doesn't want me to defend or retaliate. That's His job. He's my Defender. He is the Spear-Thrower. On the other hand, nor does He want me to become passive. It's not about being a pushover, letting the bully send me to the corner. I figure, it's somewhere between grace and doormat. "After you've done all you can, stand" (Eph. 6:13 NIV).

A Mary's heart and a David's spirit became indispensible as the spears began to fly against us.

Searching for a new location was discouraging. We would find a promising new home, only to be turned away when the landlord realized our mission was to deal with the homeless. We persevered and finally found a home in November. We were ecstatic.

The Philippine Community Society's Centre owned its building and was willing to partner with NightShift. In return, we had to complete renovations at an estimated cost of $500,000. Numbers didn't scare us. We had faith. We had seen God move. A number of homebuilders and tradespeople agreed to undertake the work as a gift-in-kind donation. We were set. After much planning, we readied ourselves to take a delegation to City Hall to present our proposal. Our hope was to gain early approval to complete partial renovations and occupy a portion of the building before the temperatures dropped.

Just when we thought we had found a new home …

Spear.

The City of Surrey and the Whalley Business Improvement Association struck. "NightShift Waits Word on Plan for Street Service," said the headline that appeared in *The Surrey Leader*, December 1, 2004. We had appeared before the City Council to ask for approval to locate our services at the Philippine Centre. Council responded, giving us an hour the following week to present our proposal—along with a related staff report.

A week later, the headline in *The Surrey Leader* read, "NightShift Closer to Having a Home." Our delegation took two hours to present a three-stage plan proposal to the City Council. At the last minute, there was an unprecedented request from Mayor Doug McCallum, who insisted that a Community Impact Statement be completed before any decisions could be reached. The impact study would examine the possible effects on the neighbouring businesses and residences.

Spear.

We were instructed to process this study, under the guidance of the City Planning Department, using its recommended consultants, before any approval to proceed would be granted. Preparing this statement was a huge additional cost for the ministry, approximately $15,000. We had received $13,000 in donations that year, which had been used to purchase food and supplies. It would be a challenge for us to raise the cash for the expense of an impact statement. However, we were prepared to do so if God prepared the means. He did. We began to prepare a Terms of Reference and Expression to five qualified consulting companies recommended by the city in order to meet with council again in the new year.

Spear.

City bylaw officials instructed us to shut down until we had a proper health license to distribute food. The headline in *The Province* newspaper, December 2004, read, "Street Ministry Says It Won't Shut Down—City Bylaw Says Surrey Group Needs License." We were bringing love, Jesus, and food to the city's poor and now we needed to get a health license to operate our street service.

Kent Spencer, *The Province* reporter, quoted me as saying, "We're not giving up. We won't break the law. Instead of soup and stew we'll give out peanut-butter-and-jelly sandwiches, or whatever we're allowed to give. People are cold and wet."

Not entirely Mary's heart. A little defiant, to be sure, and this only added more fuel to the fire of those who were trying to force us out of Whalley.

Spear.

On the day we were presenting a proposal to the city regarding approval for our new location—six months after that first meeting with the WBIA in May—the business association rose in one voice. "Mission Still Needs Business Support" reporter Ted Colley wrote in *The Surrey Now*, December 11, 2004.

"Council's response has been cautious because NightShift has done little to gain approval from area residents and local businesses," Colley wrote. "The group has alienated the 900-member Whalley Business Improvement Association because of a remark made by MaryAnne Connor, a driving force behind NightShift."

Yes, that same question and answer:

"What will you do if the community doesn't want you there?"

"We'll do it anyway."

In an interview with Pete Nichols, president of the WBIA, Colley was told that Nichols had asked me what we would do if the residents and businesses decided they didn't want NightShift in their neighbourhood. Colley wrote that my reply hadn't pleased Nichols. "They said, very adamantly, we'll do it anyway," Colley quoted Nichols. "That says a lot about the lack of co-operation and working with others."

Clearly, I had misunderstood Nichols' meaning. I had come to the WBIA seeking to assist them with their strategic plan. If they didn't want NightShift involved, fine—we'd simply continue doing what we'd started. Nichols interpreted my response as hostile and uncooperative. It was time to make amends.

God instructed me to offer an apology.

In that same article, I was quoted as saying, "I meant no disrespect. I would like to publicly apologize for that."

Finally, a Mary's heart. A David's spirit. I'd learned a lesson.

Let God throw the spears.

DISCUSSION QUESTIONS

1. **Consider the following:**
   - Joshua was a man who served faithfully. What does it mean to serve faithfully? Are you a faithful servant?
   - Do you have a Mary's heart? Why? Why not?
   - What does God say about David? Do you know anyone who exhibits a David's spirit?
   - What about you? Do you have a David's spirit?

2. **Describe a time when you responded with love and humility and not with a spear?**
   - What was the response?
   - How has this played out in your life?
   - Describe how you carry on in spite of the spears.

3. **Can Jesus' death conquer the bitterness in your heart?**
   - Can you surrender to His love?
   - What hinders you from surrender?

4. **When have you sat at God's feet and asked him to restore your heart?**
   - Are there those with whom you are angry and resentful?
   - What makes you bitter?
   - What would sweetness in your life look like?

Chapter 10

COCKROACHES

FEEDING HOMELESS CREATING problems?" This headline appeared in June 2004 in *The Surrey Leader*. Kevin Diakiw reported, "... North Surrey business owners want a group feeding the homeless to take their service elsewhere ... businesses in the area sent letters to the City appealing to officials to halt Connor's group from operating at the location...."

The WBIA's opposition to NightShift remained tireless, but while it was true their association had gathered letters of opposition from a few businesses—predominately members of the WBIA and "not in my backyard" neighbours around the corner—it was my view that these few businesses did not represent their 900-member association. They just didn't want us as neighbours.

Their complaints were appalling. One business owner accused the homeless people of defecating on the street. I ask you, given a choice, would you choose to use the sidewalk over a toilet? Remember, there wasn't much choice, apart from one public washroom in the only shelter in the area.

Diakiw reported another letter-writer as saying, "I have watched Whalley become comparable to Hasting and Main Street with drug dealers and their addicts swarming the streets like cockroaches, leaving their filth behind them, and I am protesting the allowance of drop-in centres, because these so-called homeless are drug addicts, thieves and prostitutes."

Who would call another human being a cockroach? Now that letter riled me! Need I say more?

Diakiw's story continued, "Retailers say problems in the area have worsened since Connor's group moved outdoors, and although they can't say '100 percent' that the problems are because of NightShift, they point to anecdotal evidence. Connor has heard the complaints and says the blame is misplaced. 'All they want to do is push them around like cattle.'"

I explained, "NightShift is offering food under a tarp in a city-owned green space, and business owners say it's time to move on."

My heart was sickened to see how our friends without homes were being treated, blamed, and judged. People saw the outer shell of their protective armour; we knew the softness of their broken hearts.

Abraham Maslow, an American professor of psychology, developed a theory of human motivation that lists the five hierarchical stages of man's basic needs as follows:

- Biological and Physiological Needs: air, food, drink, shelter, warmth, and sleep

- Safety Needs: protection, security, order, law, limits, stability
- Belongingness and Love Needs: family affection, relationship, work group
- Esteem Needs: achievement, status, responsibility, reputation
- Self-actualization Needs: personal growth and fulfillment

Our friends were just trying to have their basic needs met. When their next meal, shelter, and warmth needs are not met, they can't even think about hygiene, employment, respect for themselves and others, or everything else on the list.

They are not cockroaches leaving their fifth behind. They are people—like you and me. And as people, do they not deserve dignity, respect, and love? A home for someone living on the street is more than just providing four walls and a roof. It is about providing love, family, safety, and support.

I confess I've struggled with my own attitude. A close friend made a comment recently, which encapsulated exactly what I've been trying to communicate about how we regard people on the street. We see "us and them."

We were discussing local missions and the importance of helping people in our own backyards. She said, "If you can't hold hands with a homeless person in Whalley, how can you expect to go to India on a mission trip and hold someone's hand there?" How true! I have watched well-meaning volunteers pull their shirtsleeves over their hands when gathering in our prayer circle in an attempt to escape holding the hand of a street person. In truth, I've been there too. I have cringed inwardly when touching a hand so rough it felt like holding hands with a pineapple. I recall my reaction one dark night when—in our prayer circle—a hand reached out for mine in the dark. I recoiled in disgust.

In answer, I heard the Lord whisper to my spirit, "This is My hand."

I was instantly convicted and humbled beyond words. I have never looked at the hands and feet of a street person in the same way again. Instead, I remember Jesus' words, "Truly I tell you, whatever you did for one of the least of these brothers and sisters of mine, you did for me" (Matt. 25:40 NIV).

Now I look at the gnarled, black, and bruised hands and feet and wonder where they've been. What life experiences have brought them to the street? With God's compassion, I remember that Jesus didn't have a roof or a place to lay His head. His hands and feet were dirty and grimy like those of my street friends. He walked for miles on dusty roads and didn't own a bucket to draw water for drinking or bathing. This is another example of how God was using the environment He had placed me in to *shift* my attitude and open my heart to be in sympathy with His—to see people through the eyes of our Saviour.

What defines homeless people? I wrote the following article for *The Light*, a local Christian magazine, entitled,

"Dispelling the Label of Homelessness: Changing the Perceptions of 'Us and Them.'"

I set out to write about what defines "the homeless" and to present a better word to describe this group of people. After many hours assembling data on the leading causes of homelessness, how many Canadians were affected and the varied solutions recommended by the experts, I became overwhelmed, sad, and very frustrated. Much was said about the insurmountable and growing problem of homelessness, but few solutions were offered.

Society defines homelessness as "the condition of people without a regular dwelling … unable to acquire and maintain regular, safe, and adequate housing," according to Wikipedia. The US Federal Definition of Homeless is quoted as a lack of "fixed, regular, and adequate night-time residence."

But for myself, desk research has never been sufficient. I was curious as to how homeless people would describe themselves. I hit the streets of Surrey and asked Ian, one of my street friends, to help me. What came out of our brief conversation humbled me beyond words.

Ian paused for a moment, and with a smile, looked me squarely in the eyes and quoted Albert Einstein: "We can't solve our problems with the same thinking we used when we created them."

This was not what I expected to hear! Taken back, I asked him to repeat himself as the truth washed over me. The challenge of defining the word was due largely to society's perception on how we place labels on "them" —"the homeless."

"People are people—not homeless people or street people—just people!" Ian said. "Society inaccurately and unfairly labels 'them' as the homeless, poor, criminals, drug addicts, or dealers and alcoholics." As I listened to this wise man, I was quietly reminded that in the past I was guilty of doing the same. I, too, had judged and attached labels to the people on the street and segregated "them" and "us." I was part of the problem.

What would the world look like if we changed our thinking, our words, and the labels we put on people? What would it look like if we didn't isolate people as "us" and "them"? What would the world look like if we followed Jesus' words, "Do unto others as you would have them do to you?"

What if we looked at others as God looks at us? The Bible says, "The Lord does not look at the things people look at. People look at the outward appearance, but the Lord looks at the heart." God's vocabulary doesn't include labels like prostitute, addict, dealer, alcoholic, and abuser, criminal, or homeless. The words God uses for us instead include "chosen, forgiven, restored, redeemed, valuable, a masterpiece."

The irony of this is that Jesus himself was without a home. He was intentionally homeless to demonstrate humility and God's love for us. He intentionally hung out with the "least of these" to demonstrate the heavenly model of loving your neighbour as yourself and doing unto others as you would have done to you.

I recall a comment from Crissy during the early days of the shelter, "When I'm here we're all the same. There is no 'them'—it's only 'us.'" What Crissy was describing was unconditional love—the true loving of your neighbour as yourself.

This is what is at the core of dispelling terms that you wouldn't want to use for yourself. And it's a step towards easing the problems on the street.

We are "them." This is My hand.

I'm not the only one who was profoundly affected—*shifted*—through contact with the homeless. Everyone who served on the front lines of our street mission had their lives and their perceptions *shifted* at least a little. More often, the *shift* was life altering.

This is just one of the stories. It's by a volunteer, Barry Witmer, in his own words:

It was fall of 2005 and there was a chill in the air that night as I went to serve the homeless on the streets of the city of Surrey, B.C. Around me was a group of volunteers associated with NightShift Street Ministries. We were handing out food and hot drinks to the homeless. There was a table set up in the middle of the dimly lit parking lot. On it was clothing that was being given to the poor. Somewhere off to my right someone was strumming a guitar and singing a song of worship. All around us were people, those who society had rejected. They were the downcast, the broken, the addicted, and the hurting—maybe a hundred strong. They were desperate for something to eat and some warm clothes. Shopping carts loaded with all their earthly possessions were parked untidily around the outside of our serving area.

As the evening progressed, a dishevelled man appeared, pushing his cart through the crowd. It was obvious he was on drugs and he proceeded to cause quite a commotion, disrupting the peace that had settled over the crowd. He wore a heavy, army green-coloured coat. He had one shoe on and one shoe off, and was yelling and crying out as he pushed his cart through the crowd. This scene broke my heart and as I stood off to the side, I remember praying to myself, "Lord if it would be okay, please make a way for me to pray for that man tonight." The man continued on, out into the dark, past our circle of light and into the night. I thought he was gone.

A few minutes later a volunteer came up to me and tugged me on the shirt sleeve and said that there was a man who had asked for prayer and begged me to come to pray for him. I went with the volunteer—only to find the very same man who was causing the disturbance earlier in the evening. I asked him, "Can I pray with you?" (I thought that is what he wanted).

He responded with a very firm, "No!"

He said, "Praying is the last thing that I want to do!"

I was shocked and taken back by his response and slightly hurt as well. I was moved with compassion as I looked at him and just simply said, "That's fine. Could you tell me your story?"

What happened next—and the story he told—changed my life.

He said his name was Peter. When he was a young man he had accepted Christ as his Lord and Saviour. He had joined and been trained by Jack Van Impe Ministries International. He talked about evangelistic trips overseas where they told other people about Christ.

He asked me, "Do you do that thing called sowing?"

"What is sowing?" I asked.

"It's when you go door to door and tell people about Christ."

I said, "I know what you mean."

"We would do that," he said.

He described how he used to love to hear Jack Van Impe pray. He said there was no one that could pray like that man. He talked about how he adored Jack and thought so highly of him as a man of God. He paused, as though reflecting on those times, and then went on.

"I was in the southern part of the United States doing street evangelism when a guy pulled up in a car, pulled out a shot gun and shot me in the chest."

When I heard this I was thinking okay … this guy is high and is pulling my leg, this is probably not true. Then before I could react he said, "Here I'll show you." He pulled up his shirt and showed me the bullet holes in his chest. I could see what looked like maybe a half a dozen or more scarred bullet holes. My eyes grew large and I realized that the story he was telling me was true. He now had my full attention. My scepticism melted away as I listened.

He said they picked him up and threw him in the trunk of the car and drove him someplace. They opened the trunk and a man looked in and said, "You've got the wrong guy. Take him to the hospital." With that, they slammed the trunk door closed again and rushed to Emergency. They opened the trunk and dumped him on the steps to the emergency entrance. He said that they operated on him and thankfully he survived, but some of the bullet fragments were so close to his heart that the doctor was unable to remove them without doing more damage.

Over the next season of time as he recovered, the pain was excruciating. He had to take painkillers in order to cope. It was during this time he became addicted to prescription drugs. As he talked, he fumbled around in his coat pocket with one hand and leaned on the grocery cart with the other. He dropped a bottle of prescription drugs on the ground and was in no hurry to pick them up. He continued the story.

He had a beautiful wife, he said, but she left him years ago because of his drug problem. Today he had received news that his teenage daughter had given up on life and committed suicide.

As he relived the story he became overcome with deep grief. I watched as he crumpled to the ground and knelt down on the little strip of grass between the sidewalk and King George Highway. He sobbed and cried with the most gut-wrenching, searing pain.

I knelt down beside him and asked if I could pray for him now and he said, "Sure."

I just uttered a simple prayer, maybe three sentences, because he had already told me that he didn't want to pray and I didn't want to offend him. When I had finished speaking, to my amazement, the man began to pray himself.

What happened next, I have never experienced before or since. I have grown up around churches, prayer meetings, and Christians but what happened there on the sidewalk of King George Highway that night will stay with me for life.

As this man prayed, the residue from the medication just seemed to melt away. He transformed before my eyes. He was completely sober. His mind was clear. His face was transformed from that of a drug addict to that of a forgiven child of God. When he prayed, it was like heaven opened and there was direct access into the throne room of God. He prayed with such raw humility and sincerity unlike anything that I had ever seen in or out of the church.

He began by repenting of the fact that he had not been a very good husband to his wife and asked the heavenly father to please forgive him and be merciful. He asked for forgiveness for not being a good father to his daughter during the previous years. He continued to pray and cry out to God confessing his sins and then worshipping God for about ten minutes. What struck me about this time was the fact that he knew beyond a shadow of doubt that God knew him and loved him and hadn't abandoned him in spite of all he had been through.

At the end of this time he said, "Oh, Barry, a few minutes ago, praying was the last thing that I wanted to do, but now I don't want to stop."

The moment was holy.

We finished and stood up. We said good-bye. We each went different ways, he into the night pushing his cart; I back to the team of volunteers. Night after night I would search the crowd looking for his face. As the various teams served on the streets week in and week out, I would enquire if anyone had seen Peter. I wanted to know how he was doing, and where he was, but I never saw him again.

I don't know what happened to him after that night. I don't know if he lived or died. He simply disappeared. I nicknamed him "Peter the Rock" because I wanted to impart something positive to encourage him to hold on.

The "Peters" of the world are the type of people that heaven loves to welcome. Not just a handshake and then shown through heaven's gate. No, I see the King running toward the gate, face full of joy. A full embrace, a twirl sweeping the Peters off their feet. A party begins, and then a parade with balloons, confetti, music, and dancing.

The lost is found!
Tears of joy!
His favourite is home again!

Peter has no idea the impact his story had on me that night. My stereotypical image shattered. My heart broken for the poor. One day, I'll tell him.

One day.

DISCUSSION QUESTIONS

1. **What would the world look like…**
   - If we changed our thinking, our words, and the labels we put on people?

2. **Do you see unfortunate people as 'them'?**
   - What does it mean to think of people as 'us' not 'them'?
   - Do you have a 'them' and 'us' attitude?

3. **How do you look at people?**
   - How does this form your judgment of people before you even speak to them?
   - What labels do you use to describe people?
   - What labels have others used about you?
   - What would it take for you to remove these labels?
   - Are you able to shift your judgment of someone? How? What would happen?

4. **What would be different if we loved unconditionally?**

5. **Have you ever experienced the power of prayer?**
   - How did it impact or change you?
   - What does it mean to you?

Chapter 11

STRUGGLE

JUST IN TIME for Christmas, on December 24, 2004, *The Province* newspaper ran a story by Kent Spencer.

"The NightShift ministry does not have the official blessing of Surrey Council," Spencer reported. "Businesses and residences complain there are too many social services already in the area."

Once again, another newspaper story had suggested to the public that the Surrey Council, businesses, and residences did not condone us. "Too many social services ..." Really? I thought of Dr. Seuss and wondered how the spear-carriers were enjoying their "roast beast" dinners this holiday season. Yes, I know, too Marah of me.

"Then the Grinch thought of something he hadn't before.
What if Christmas, he thought, doesn't come from a store.
What if Christmas, perhaps, means a little bit more."

But in the newspaper story there was a glimmer of hope, "… but Surrey bylaw offices have left the kitchen alone," the newspaper reported.

We were okay. We could still feed the poor. We knew we had God's blessing. And there was a silver lining to this dark cloud.

Night after night, a bylaw vehicle pulled up slowly, parked nearby, and closely monitored our operation. Apparently, people had been complaining that we were leaving garbage behind; worse still, that we were also permitting people to use drugs. Ironically, God used the bylaw department's close scrutiny to defend us. John Sherstone, manager of Licensing and Bylaws at the time of this surveillance, confided to me years later that when people called to complain that we were creating a mess, he was able to respond truthfully that Bylaws was aware firsthand that this was not the case. He appreciated the fact we did every single thing that we had promised to do.

Sherstone began to trust my word and honour. He ultimately became our first ally in the city's bureaucracy. Did anyone ever mention that God works in mysterious ways?

We moved into a new year and celebrated the first anniversary of NightShift. But with the city's deadline upon us—we still needed the city's okay for a new location and approval from the health department to continue our service—we knew we had a lot of work on our hands to break down barriers.

The press had quoted Mayor Doug McCallum, saying: "NightShift's proposal has been rejected in the absence of a Community Impact Study. Once they have done that and they submit it to council, then we'll look at their project but my understanding is that they don't have the support."

He had continued, "I suspect that council will turn down their application."

We tried not to be disheartened but I found these comments puzzling. How would the mayor know if we could or would not gain public support? We hadn't presented our proposal to the residents, businesses, or WBIA. The opposition that the mayor referred to was based on his opinion and hearsay; it was unsupported by factual information.

By now we believed that our future shelter was somewhere out there on the horizon. Despite the wounds of a few battles and false accusations to discourage us, we were not forsaken. But there was more to come.

We had we been falsely accused of operating illegally; we were opposed by the city, the WBIA, and supposedly the entire community; now the Food Bank was quoted as stating they were considering retracting their support of NightShift because we didn't have the health department's approval to serve meals.

We kept going with our do-it-anyway mantra.

We were now meeting regularly with our nightly team leaders, made up of key people who led a night or multiple nights every week. At the same time, our board, established to meet on a monthly basis, now met almost weekly, sometimes daily. We had much to discuss, lots of planning to finish, and a lot of opposition to contend with.

The Surrey Now newspaper published a story that described the homeless as the "underbelly of society" and voiced the concerns of the mayor and a few businesses regarding NightShift's continued operation under the headline, "Food Bank May Sever NightShift Ties."

On January 26, 2005, Now Reporter Marisa Babic quoted the mayor as saying "NightShift is operating without proper city and health permits and has been warned that if they continue to flout the rules, that the City will close them down. It's only fair to give them a warning that they have to have proper permits to do it. They do not have those permits and eventually we will shut them down. We've given them warning and we're working through that process," McCallum said.

The truth is the city never inspected NightShift nor did we receive any warnings that we were operating without proper permits—apart from those we were reading in the local newspapers along with the rest of the community. The allegations that we were operating illegally were never substantiated, but the damage was done. Our public image was tainted. We were thought of as flouting the rules, disrespecting the community, and I was a rebel leader.

Once again, it was time for a Mary's heart.

I arranged a meeting with the city's manager of By-Law and Licensing Services and the manager of Fraser Health Authority. Both were made aware of our desire to operate within the legal boundaries of the city and health department. We were prepared to comply with any city or health permits should they prove we were operating inappropriately. Bylaws and Planning were cautiously cooperative and willing to work with us.

The fact is no one had ever identified any areas that substantiated we were operating outside the limits of the law. Bad PR or not, if the opposition expected us to give up after a year of battle, they were wrong. We pressed on.

Good news came in the form of a dilapidated old U-built trailer, which was donated through a member of a local church. It limped. It was a cast-off no one else wanted, but it was a castle to me.

Our intention was to equip a mobile kitchen that would enable us to serve food in a safe and healthy environment. Our volunteer team was continuing to faithfully serve in the dark, cold, and wet weather on Bentley Field. We were hoping to have the trailer on the road within a few weeks. It would serve as a temporary solution for our street operation if the shelter, as we had envisioned it, became a reality somewhere down the road.

As I began to look for a way to have the trailer renovated, God provided. Renovations began when a homebuilder helped to coordinate the work and underwrote the cost for the kitchen upgrades. We were ready to hit the road.

There were still many challenges to overcome. The ministry was stretched to heights we'd never imagined. God was faithful and provided for every need. Our street friends were asking for prayer, receiving Jesus, and taking steps towards a better life. Many were finding jobs, shelter, and moving into recovery programs.

But the struggle continued—for "them" and "us."

The WBIA, determined to push through its mandate of removing us from Whalley, conducted its own impact study. The survey was distributed to a chosen number of their members and asked questions concerning the homeless situation in Whalley.

I was struggling to accept that the concerns and opposition expressed by a very small number of businesses and residents in Whalley really echoed the voice of the entire community. There was a solution for this crisis: shouldn't everyone in Surrey have a voice and be given the opportunity to get involved?

We prayed that these surveys and forums would provide the avenue for citizens and businesses to speak up. Perhaps they would reveal the answers to some of the many questions we had been pursuing in our Community Impact Study. Our board had made the decision to stop the process on our infamous Community Impact Study because—after the mayor's statement that he suspected the council would turn down our application—we believed it was futile to move forward on this front. It made no sense to spend the time and money when we faced probable rejection. NightShift didn't have the finances to waste on a study that appeared to be defeated before its completion.

Next, there were concerns about the duplication and concentration of services in the city core by our friends from the Food Bank, the City of Surrey, and the WBIA. What these groups didn't understand was that NightShift offered a unique service on a consistent nightly basis. Outside. Regardless of the weather. 365 days a year. Other service providers in the Whalley area did not duplicate this. We were reaching out in a very different way.

Another important difference is that we are not funded by government dollars. We operate solely through volunteer support and donations. The Food Bank and our other critics also didn't acknowledge that NightShift does more than distribute food. We also provide love, street counsellors, prayer, and encouragement to those in need—as well as regularly referring people to social services and recovery homes. This is not a job to our volunteers. It is a ministry, designed by God to transform lives.

In spite of the opposition, we continued to express our desire and willingness to work with different groups to find a common solution to the need. We were rarely made to feel welcome to the table.

I took a ton of heat back then for these articles that were being published. Just reading them again raises my blood pressure.

Heat came not just from the press but also from some of the volunteers serving with us. Many were working long hours, freely giving of themselves, and sacrificing time to do all they could to love our street friends. They questioned why all the attention was directed at me. But I hadn't encouraged these stories, not one. They just happened. And they continued to happen. It was like God had flipped the breaker. The floodlights exploded. The envy and resentment surfacing from some of my colleagues—as well as from the Surrey community—became awkward. I felt like a target on everyone's radar screen.

As spears were grasped, aimed, and thrown, I knew deep down that these stories weren't about me. It was God who was behind them. I was just "the face." He reminded me of this regularly. He had just parachuted me in. The stories had a greater purpose.

The stories communicated a message. God. Love. Hope. Care. They spoke of God's heart for the poor and the broken. They called for social justice. They caused people to search their own hearts for their prejudices and stigmas they had perhaps placed on the "lepers" of society. The stories stirred the pot. Anger. Resentment. They challenged people to step up to the plate and get involved. Even today, eight years later, people continue to be drawn to information sessions at the ministry, inspired by that *Surrey Leader* article of January 23, 2004, when reporter Kevin Diakiw wrote the first piece about NightShift and told me, "You're the story."

"God had a plan and a purpose" (Jer. 29:11 NIV).

God also taught me about taking offences and holding on to them as resentments, judgments, and unforgiveness—bitterness that could seep back into my Mary's heart. God used John Bevere to reveal some of what I was finding unforgivable. In his book *The Bait of Satan*, Bevere talks about how the devil's most effective scheme against us is to lure God's people into taking offence, as if it were bait. I was being hooked on a regular basis. The spears hit, and I took offence. Worse, I held on to them! My anger sometimes made me such an easy target.

If I didn't pull out the spears and drop them quickly, I was in whopping trouble. They would become ugly resentments, which would develop into bitter roots of judgment and unforgiveness—Satan's deadly bait, his ultimate weapon.

Time and again, my anger kept me from receiving God's forgiveness and effectively blocked my intimacy with Him. Time and again, I was on my knees, confessing and repenting and asking for His forgiveness.

Those two revelations—David's struggles and not taking the bait—have been pivotal for my spiritual health and my leadership training. And I am tested regularly. Thankfully, God is slowly changing my heart—one day at a time, one spear at a time.

DISCUSSION QUESTIONS

1. **Do you know how community services are funded where you live?**
   - Do you believe in tithing? Financial donating?
   - Do you tithe? Donate?

2. **Are you prepared for the 'spears'?**
   - Have you ever experienced 'spears' in your life?
   - What were they?
   - How were they overcome?

3. **What is a 'good Samaritan'?**
   - Can you become a 'good Samaritan'?
   - Who is your ally in your service/ministry/personal life?
   - Would you consider them a 'good Samaritan'? Why?
   - How are you going to get involved and make a difference?

Chapter 12

FLANKED

I WAS GETTING accustomed to the resistance from the City of Surrey and the angry assaults by the WBIA— I'd never get used to cruel letters calling people cockroaches—but I was completely caught off guard by the surprising reaction of a few established church leaders of our community.

In strategic terms, it would be fair to say I had been outflanked: the people I most trusted to "have my back" were, in fact, undermining NightShift, particularly my leadership in the organization.

You have to understand this was 2005, NightShift was only a year in the making, we were the upstart "ragamuffins," people were still uncertain of my motives and my commitment, our press was unfavourable, and we were seen by some as radicals battling civic and business authority. Over the years, these negatives have been greatly resolved and our relationship with the church community is well established. But back then I had as much struggle with the politics of the local church ministerial association as I did with the city.

The story of NightShift wouldn't be complete without this account. Certainly I've spent a lot of time with God about how and whether or not to reveal this chapter. Let me try to be as fair and balanced as I can about it.

The local ministerial association consists of pastors from several churches within Surrey. They meet weekly to pray, discuss, promote, and when necessary, deal with church business in the community. It would be an omission for me not to mention that historically it was unusual for a woman to lead a ministry such as NightShift, and in truth, in some denominations, women were generally discouraged from stepping into lead pastoral roles and very few spoke from the pulpit. Today, there are woman pastors (including me) and women play increasingly higher profile roles in our churches. But you can see how, back then, some conflict could arise on gender issues alone: I was, after all, a woman, and some people have suggested I can be a little assertive.

Well, actually they have used the term "pushy," but on reflection, I remember trying to be submissive and humble when dealing with the church leaders. My view was: because they were pastors, they were close to God and I could trust them. Later, I came to realize that pastors—like most everyone—have their own issues. It was a huge awakening for me.

I approached the ministerial association to enlist their prayer support and blessing on the advice of one of the pastors in my home church, and was granted permission to present NightShift to the executive team. Our prayer was that all the churches in Surrey would work alongside each other with NightShift in helping to bring about much-needed social change in our community.

I brought along a well-rehearsed and visually attractive PowerPoint presentation, eager to introduce NightShift to the church leaders. It never got played. The meeting, it turned out, was almost as unfriendly as the one I had encountered with the WBIA. I felt as if I were being interviewed to work with the association. A woman. No ministry background. Creating nothing but bad press in the community. I felt like the proverbial deer caught in the headlights. Again, just like that of the WBIA, the response was so unexpected, I just wasn't prepared. (Yes, I know, for some of God's slower pupils, the lesson has to be repeated.)

One positive opportunity arose from our meetings: we were invited to present NightShift to the three multi-denominational services at the Chandos Pattison Pavilion, an annual event organized by the association. We had a booth and, for the first time, three thousand people—the *body* of the church—had the opportunity to meet us. The exposure was amazing as well as humbling. Our booth drew many people who were excited about what we were doing and wanted to know how they could become involved. The positive response inspired our inaugural bi-monthly information sessions for people who wanted to serve in street ministry.

NightShift, in its rough-around-the-edges way, was doing what the ministerial association strived to do—bring together people from all congregations, the body of the church—in a coordinated effort to serve Christ and assist people struggling with poverty and homelessness in our community. Even then, we had over sixty volunteers from ten churches. Today, we have a database of volunteers and supporters of 2,500. For the ministerial association back then, it must have been a little like how MySpace felt about Facebook.

To be fair, it was true that NightShift—particularly at that time—was generating lots of negative press, locally and city-wide, and that was reflecting poorly on the work of other charities of Christian churches in Surrey, the very thing the ministerial association was established to monitor. We were seen as being disrespectful to the wishes of the city and the business community. The backlash was so negative that at one point a pastor from the association was dismissed by Mayor McCallum from the police committee simply because the pastor was known to have an association with NightShift.

In certain circles, we were social lepers ourselves.

The executive team of the ministerial association walked alongside us throughtout 2005 with City Planning, team meetings, and addressing various board governance issues. The solution, it appeared, was to remove me from NightShift's board and relegate me to executive director or some similar employee status, a position presumably from which I could be eventually dismissed and my influence permanently removed from the ministry. At one point, there was a meeting with some members of the association with Mayor McCallum to discuss NightShift and the Philippine Community Centre, a meeting I was not invited to. This was a confusing and painful time for me. My leadership was under scrutiny and questioned. And through it all, my faith was shaken and under attack.

However, I did have Someone to turn to.

As it happens, a month earlier, Pastor Steve Witmer of the Bible Fellowship Foursquare Church had preached a New Year's message about the great prophet Elisha and Jehoash, king of Israel. In a war between Israel and Syria (2 Kings 13:18 NIV), Elisha instructed King Jehoash to get a bow and some arrows and shoot them in faith through an open window to the east at the enemy. The arrows signified God's deliverance—the arrows of victory. King Jehoash did not receive Elisha's instructions whole-heartedly. Instead, he timidly shot the arrow at no particular target. Elisha exhorted the king to "strike the ground"—to pound the ground vehemently—but the king struck the ground only three times.

"You should have struck the ground five or six times," Elisha reprimanded the king, saying now victory would be incomplete. As Pastor Witmer explained, the king gave up instead of "striking" the ground enough times to ensure success.

God spoke to my heart through this message. I was encouraged not to give up in spite of the opposition that faced me from all sides. NightShift needed to "strike the ground" and keep striking until we experienced a break-through. It was not the time to give up. In fact, it was the exact opposite. This was the time for us to trust God. Time to give Him our all and to press forward in faith.

For more than a year, the pressure on me to give up my leadership role in NightShift was persistent. It began with an internal report to the ministerial association written by its advisory consultant, who was appointed to assist NightShift. He advised that only one of the five NightShift board members was "worth keeping" and that I would be willing to step down from the board and get out of the line of fire as long as NightShift didn't stop serving our street family. This was erroneous on both counts.

Soon after, I met with this advisor along with a newly appointed NightShift board member. To my dismay, this board member announced that he had received a message from God through his personal scripture reading. God's message was to "lay down the sword."

I was advised to give up pursuing both the shelter and the Community Impact Statement required by the city. I was stunned! This was exactly the opposite of the word that God had given me in 2 Kings 13—to pound the ground and forge ahead.

For an hour, I listened to their appeal to "lay down the sword" and retreat. This advice came from my own colleagues, people for whom I had a great deal of respect and openheartedness. Now what should I do?

We were up against powerful political resistance, a strong-voiced, influential business association, and now even our own church establishment. Our team was becoming tired and discouraged. Things looked impossible. A shelter? Not in your dreams. An impact statement? With whose money? Spiritually and physically, the enemy was wearing us down.

This was a typical Goliath situation (1 Sam. 17:1-58). We were up against a powerful enemy, and like David, we were minuscule in comparison to its stature. The real enemy? Money and politics! It was obvious that the "not in my backyard" mindset was alive and well in Whalley. Housing and business development plans were underway. There were high-rise condominiums, townhome developments, and future business expansions to be built. Quite frankly, the poor and homeless were roadblocks to these strategies. A new vision for the city and million dollar fortunes were at stake. Who were we to stand in the way? What even gave us the right to stand against progress? I used to be in real estate. Who better to understand the forces at play?

What to do? "Strike the ground" or "lay down the sword?"

I spent considerable time in prayer and devotions scouring through His Word for confirmation. Time and time again, His Word encouraged me to advance, not to retreat. God had spoken clearly to me about how He wanted us to treat those suffering in poverty in our community, "There will always be poor people in the land. Therefore I command you to be open-handed towards your brothers and toward the poor and needy" (Deut. 15:11 NIV).

The choice was obvious: the shelter was not going to become a reality without a fight.

In my heart, I knew that in God's timing He would provide a roof over our heads. I was certain that He wanted us to endure in faith, even if that meant continuing to serve the poor and homeless in inclement weather until it materialized. Little did I know it would take another long year for it to become a reality.

But the incessant spear throwing—from all directions— had taken its toll on me. My faith was feeling the stabs. It was increasingly more difficult to hold my head high in the face of such intense opposition. I turned to God and began carefully searching His Word for help. My dining room table became my Bible school. I dug. I studied. I learned. My faith grew and deepened. Amongst many scriptures, I discovered Joshua and the Lord's commands to him after he was installed as leader following the death of Moses.

God told Joshua to be strong and of good courage. He was speaking the same to me.

> Be strong and courageous. Be careful to obey all the law my servant Moses gave you; do not turn from it to the right or to the left, that you may be successful where you go. Keep this Book of the Law always on your lips; meditate on it day and night, so that you may be careful to do everything in it. Then you will be prosperous and successful.
>
> —Joshua 1:7-8 NIV

Encouraged, I made a commitment to follow God's instructions carefully. I trusted that He would walk with me through to victory. He delivered precisely what I asked of Him—His guidance, wisdom, and discernment. He promised to be with me wherever I went with the assurance that I need not be frightened of any resistance. He urged me to keep my eyes on Him and not to be discouraged: "Have

I not commanded you? Be strong and courageous. Do not be afraid; do not be discouraged, for the LORD your God will be with you wherever you go" (Josh. 1:9 NIV).

He explicitly instructed me to "love the Lord your God with all your heart and with all your soul and with all your mind and with all your strength" (Mark 12:30 NIV). Three letters—"all"—resonated to the very depths of my soul. Love Him not with "some" of my heart, soul, mind, and strength. But with "*all*"! He wanted my "all"—all I had within me. No compromise. Full measure. The revelation of this steadied me. It was as if He set a rod of iron in my spine. With a new resolve, I straightened up, squared my shoulders, shook off discouragement and fear, and stepped head on into battle. I refused to be derailed. I wasn't alone. God was with me.

"Strike the ground."

There came the day when, at a meeting with the ministerial association, I boldly, but assuredly said, "I don't know who told you guys that you're my big brothers, but you're not, and you're not sending me to the corner anymore."

Try as they might, those members of the church establishment who wanted the NightShift board expanded to include a member of their executive team did not succeed. It was a prolonged and painful episode—one that I'm happy is now well behind us—but in the end NightShift held together and persevered. Today, we have unity with the churches of Surrey and with the church ministerial association. We represent what the church leaders had so long envisioned and wanted to create within the community: the movement that brought unity to the body of the church, regardless of denomination or church affiliation, to serve the poor and homeless in Surrey.

In the end, did it really matter which group accomplished that purpose? The beautiful story is that—for the good of all—it happened with so many churches and so many Christians coming together as one to serve Christ.

As God promised,

So if you faithfully obey the commands I am giving you today—to love the LORD your God and to serve him with all your heart and with all your soul—then I will send rain on your land in its season, both autumn and spring rains, so that you may gather in your grain, new wine and olive oil. I will provide grass in the fields for your cattle, and you will eat and be satisfied.

—Deuteronomy 11:13-15 NIV

DISCUSSION QUESTIONS

1. **Do you expect your clergy to be perfect role models?**
   - How do you feel about working with any minister after you see his or her 'feet of clay'?

2. **Do you give up too easily?**
   - What would it take for you to not give up? To 'strike the ground' until you experienced break through?
   - Likewise, do you quit too soon – even when in your heart you feel God's will? Why did you give up?
   - Describe when you have endured in faith.
   - God encourages us to be strong and courageous and not be discouraged. Can you respond with courage?

3. **Do you love God with all your heart?**
   - How do you know God is with you?
   - What can you do to strengthen your love for God?

Chapter 13

LAWBREAKERS

T RUSTING GOD FOR provision, I made the inevitable decision to step into full-time ministry in February 2005.

The first thing I needed was an office, a place where I could establish a filing, accounting, and database system. In my previous life as a real estate princess, I had staff do such tasks. Clearly, life had changed. I set up a temporary office in the basement of my little rented cottage and took the first step on what felt like an insurmountable mountain of organizational work. This was not my gift, but with the guidance of the Holy Spirit, we began to craft what eventually became a primitive, bare-bones administration system. And I mean *bare-bones*. Here I was in the cold, damp basement with my computer, a desk, a filing cabinet and a bookcase from my former business, a couple lamps, a phone, my two beloved golden retrievers, Gracie (who had come back to live with me) and Lucy, at my feet. I had my dogs, my office, and the mould. I had come a long way, baby!

With the basics under way, I thought we should buckle down and get serious about finding a space in Whalley for an administration office and storage. The mould was beginning to get to me. I hit the streets looking for a spot.

The media hadn't erupted for a while, the WBIA and the city weren't currently on the attack, and we thought maybe the opposition had settled down. Then, bang! We were blindsided again. This time by a very powerful player.

The Fraser Health Authority contacted me and insisted on a meeting. I complied and brought along the builder who was coordinating the renovations on the U-built trailer as our new mobile kitchen. The meeting was a disaster. Fraser Health refused to give us a permit to serve hot meals. Our dinner service was shut down. Just like that. Done.

We were given a crumb, a permit to serve peanut-butter-and-jelly sandwiches, but until we had a kitchen approved and licensed by Fraser Health Authority, there would be no hot meals. Our mobile kitchen would take months to complete.

Can you imagine?

This was a huge setback. On most nights our serving line-up had swollen to one hundred people—one hundred *hungry* people. No other social provider was serving a hot meal on a consistent basis. Peanut-butter-and-jelly sandwiches just wouldn't cut it.

As my critics say, I can be a little assertive. Thank goodness in this case, because I couldn't accept peanut-butter-and-jelly sandwiches for an answer, not for the hundred homeless people who counted on NightShift. I pressed for a compromise. After considerable arm-wrestling—and, yes, a few raised voices—I walked away with a grudging approval to include hotdogs on the menu. Victory! I was elated.

That is, until I got to my car.

Then it hit me. What was I thinking? Seven hundred people a week times seven hundred hotdogs, what's that going to cost us? I knew the answer. Huge bucks. We didn't have a dime in the coffers. Do you know what pyrrhic victory is? It's a victory with such a devastating cost to the victor that it ultimately causes defeat. I was the living, breathing example. Nice going, girl.

Smacked straight in the face with a bucket of cold water, discouraged, my short-lived elation thoroughly drenched, I hoped God had a plan.

The next morning, I met over coffee with one of our nightly team leaders who helped coordinate our food and supplies. His phone rang in the middle of my review of the dismal Fraser Health Authority meeting. He put the phone to his ear, listened for a second, covered his hand over the mouthpiece and asked me, "Can we use any smokies?" I hesitated for a second. I asked myself, "Would smokies be on the same shelf as hot dogs in the grocery store?" My answer, "I think so." I nodded yes. Within seconds, he was back with another question. With a puzzled look on his face, he asked, "Can we use four thousand pounds?"

Can we? Are you kidding me?

When God provides, He provides. "If you help the poor, you are lending to the LORD—and He will repay you" (Prov. 19:17 NIV). What a payback. Wow!

I was back. Elation!

Smokies were served every single night for four months until June 30, 2005, when our spanking almost brand-new retrofitted kitchen was deployed. Smokies, every night. Served every imaginable way we could think of! With fancy condiments. Cheese. Sauerkraut. Chili. You name it. Our street friends loved it. Imagine eating smokies every night for four months. Maybe not, but not one person complained. It was a miracle that brought much joy to our team. We needed the encouragement. Hallelujah!

God had our attention. If He could miraculously provide smokies, what other unimaginable things would He provide? That was just the beginning. How I love that "smokie" story. We still chuckle about it today.

Things continued to look up. We still had the ongoing internal struggle with the ministry association, but by March, the negative press about NightShift had disappeared. In complete contrast, *The Surrey Now* published a cover and centre-page story, "Soul Food For Surrey's Hungry—NightShift's MaryAnne Connor left a six-figure salary to feed the poor." The centre page spread displayed a positive report and photographs on the ministry. Marisa Babic, staff reporter, wrote,

MaryAnne Connor has thrown the good life away for the Good Book. Connor used to earn a six-figure salary and mingle with the movers and shakers of this world.

But a life-altering experience prompted her to throw it all away. That was the beginning of the "shift." Connor is unapologetic about serving up a helping of the gospel along the way with soup. The meal begins with grace and everyone bows their heads. "Amen!" the crowd rejoins enthusiastically, as the soup line begins to move. The evening ends with a prayer circle in which each person is invited to place their right hand on the shoulder of the person next to them and bow their heads in prayer.

We were pumped. Things were happening. In May, we finally received a Fraser Health Authority permit to operate a soup kitchen. We were saddened to learn that Pastor Steen had to stop serving with our nightly teams due to health reasons but happy that he could stay on as our street pastor as needed. And then, the best news of all: we found the perfect office space on 108th Avenue, just a few blocks away from where we served. We entered into a two-year lease and submitted plans for a building permit.

Great plans. Then *wham!* The city struck again.

Spear.

A new bylaw appeared overnight. It prohibited non-profits from conducting community services in the City Centre. The bylaw didn't have our name on it, but otherwise it was all ours. No business license for us. At least not until we had a Community Impact Statement approved by City Council.

Angry? I was steaming.

We were stopped dead in our tracks. All the fuss about the mayor saying we didn't have community support came back to me. And if we submitted an impact study, as required by City Planning, what was the likelihood we would obtain approval from City Council? Remember what Mayor McCallum said? "I suspect that Council will turn down their application." Right. I'm not generally that suspicious, but to be truthful, I was thinking we were getting the City Hall shaft.

I tried to manoeuvre around the bylaw, citing we were using the space for administration purposes and warehousing only. Further, I promised we would not be cooking dinner on the premises or serving the homeless people out of the building. That was the truth. But City Hall came back with, "Because you are thinking about doing that, and (heaven forbid!) organizing volunteers to do community service, the answer is still no."

We couldn't afford the time or the money to chase after an impact study. We believed we wouldn't have received community or council's approval anyway. We were stymied.

So we pulled back into the cocoon like a caterpillar, resting in the chrysalis stage of development. It didn't matter how much we pecked, we weren't going to spread our wings and fly until God thought we were ready. We had to have faith: He was allowing these things to happen for a reason.

But while we stepped back, the city took another step forward.

Spear.

Even though we had obtained the necessary health permits and an approved license from Fraser Health

Authority, the city's bylaw department would not issue a business license for our newly renovated mobile kitchen.

We found a way around that obstacle but it required that we locate a business owner who would agree to let us park our mobile kitchen and serve the homeless on that owner's property. No matter who we talked to, no one wanted to touch us with a ten-foot pole. So even though we had done our utmost to comply with all the city's regulations, we were banned again from helping people who were hungry.

Writing about this now makes my blood pressure rise again. Things were beyond ridiculous. Whoever was behind all of this should be ashamed.

Forced to operate without a license was not our preference. But the need was great. And we put lives first before red tape. If the only way we could operate was illegally, then we all agreed: we accepted the consequences. We would break the law.

DISCUSSION QUESTIONS

1. Are you prepared for a life-altering experience?

- Have you experienced life-altering moments? Explain.

2. Are you prepared for defeat?

- How do you combat defeat? What does God say about being defeated?
- When you are defeated how do you respond? How does God respond?

3. Is it ok to break the law in the name of God?

- Why?
- Why not?

Chapter 14

ISRAELITES

THAT SUMMER AT Bentley Field, we carried on seven nights a week serving hot meals without approval or permission.

In contravention of city bylaws, the homeless appeared in the summer night, gave thanks to God, ate the one good meal they had a day, and joined us hand-in-hand in prayer. Souls were reached by the Christian volunteers and some left their addictions behind to move to detox centres and recovery homes. Most could not yet make that journey but they had one certainty they could count on: they knew we would be there for them.

But a resident whose home was adjacent to Bentley Field began to voice his concerns—persistent and very loud concerns—about NightShift's outreach. He blamed us for bringing homeless people all the way from Vancouver for dinner.

Our dinners must have a great reputation on the street, I thought, but of course this was not happening. No one was taking the Skytrain from the Downtown Eastside to dine at Bentley Field.

We had been serving the homeless in the field for almost a year, so we couldn't complain. We were grateful for the gracious, kind-hearted neighbours who had looked the other way. However, given our tenuous circumstances with the law, we were forced to move on.

The problem was: we didn't have a clue where to go next.

We were like the Israelites, on the move again. In our case, our wilderness was Whalley. Then we found refuge in an unlikely place. The Mennonite Central Committee (MCC) had a thrift store on King George Highway. They were approached to see if they had an appetite to permit us to serve from their massive parking lot. After all, we were all on the same team, weren't we? The Mennonites agreed: we were.

The location had an added bonus. Not only were we operating legally again, but it also provided us with electricity for lighting and running the equipment the worship teams used. Oh, happy day! In July, we moved our operations to our new spot. We set up every night after business hours, tucked in the front entrance of MCC, barely visible from the main roadway. For a while we were happy campers. Gateway Baptist Church gave us permission to use their parking lot to park our truck and mobile kitchen. We still park them there today.

Things were going well, but just to the side of the MCC parking lot was Beamriders, a sound and video business.

They were experts at installing car audio systems but they weren't big proponents of brotherly love.

Even though we served our friends after business hours, Beamriders wasn't thrilled about us operating in the adjacent parking lot. Every night, Beamriders would blast heavy metal music from speakers on its awning to drown out our worship music. The owner of the building filed a formal complaint with the MCC, RCMP, WBIA, and City of Surrey regarding our evening service. We weren't invited to any of these meetings nor given the opportunity to respond to the allegations. The Beamriders building was up for sale, the owner was desperate, and we weren't helping her agenda.

Soon we were accused once again of leaving garbage behind, encouraging drugs and—well, you know, all the usual complaints. Frankly, we were getting pretty tired of hearing the same blah-blah-blah. It was getting old. We were fastidious about cleanup. In fact, every night, our homeless friends helped with garbage pickup to keep the parking lot clean. It was our intent to help people with addictions get off the street. We never tolerated drug use in our presence. But none of that mattered. Within a month, we were forced out by City of Surrey Bylaws.

I know it hardly compares to forty years in the wilderness, but sometimes it felt that way. We'd lost the battle twice over securing a new building. We had moved twice in under a year. Now what? Winter was around the bend. It wasn't looking good.

It tested our faith, but we trusted God. The Whalley chapter of the Israelites was on the move again.

I remember the night we were told to move on, standing outside of the Beamriders building. I remember how frustrated I felt, staring at it.

I asked God, "Could we have that building?"

Then two angels rescued us. They wore RCMP uniforms and I came to know them well. (One lost the battle fighting cancer and went home to be with the Lord; his faithful wife still comes out to the NightShift street ministry every Friday night with a group of students from a Catholic school in Abbotsford.) They were police officers with God-shaped, Christ-filled hearts, but you couldn't fool me: I know they were really angels.

These two men searched every nook and cranny in Whalley to find us a place to serve that wouldn't negatively affect the business or residential community. I don't think Mayor McCallum ever knew what they were doing behind the scenes to help us. It's the reason I don't mention their names, for their names are etched in my heart. Maybe I'm being paranoid, but I felt that there was much covert malevolence going on at the time. I'm still afraid that repercussions might follow if I revealed their identities. Needless to say, I think there's a huge reward waiting for them in heaven.

Two other friends of NightShift whose names I can reveal abetted them. The first was John Sherstone, now retired but then the manager of Bylaw and Licensing Services for the

City of Surrey. Remember, it was his staff who watched us at Bentley Field to ensure we weren't breaking the conditions of the bylaw and saw how we and our homeless friends cleaned up the field every night and that there was no drug-taking or mischief. We had earned Sherstone's trust.

Sherstone, a former RCMP Staff Sergeant, upon retiring from that position, joined the City of Surrey to administer their bylaws and licensing. Both his department and the RCMP had the authority to roust us out of Dodge completely—but they didn't. Given the animosity that surrounded NightShift, they showed a lot of goodwill and courage.

Let me add to that one other name—Whalley Staff Sergeant Barry Hickman. Hickman was a great guy. I used to tease him by calling him Pastor Hickman because he was so kind in his way to the street people. The staff sergeant and I had our differences, but we respected and worked with each other.

Imagine—the authorities were actually extending us a helping hand. What does that say for God? And for tenacity? The way I see it, all these men were miraculously used by God to fulfill His purposes.

I think of the song by my friend Andy Park, the acclaimed worship artist, who sings about the Wonder-Working God:

Our loving Father
We know You are here
We bring You our worries and all of our fears
We bring You the problems that we cannot solve
We know You are faithful

We know you are strong
Wonder-working God, open the heavens
You can make a way where there is no way
Wonder-working God, you can move mountains
You can make a way right here today

Working together, these four men found us the perfect place—on 107th Avenue, tucked out of sight from traffic and prying eyes.

Then donations started to pour in.

Seven churches united together to raise a "Mountain of Food" for Thanksgiving, and we needed a storage place. Remember how we weren't allowed one in Whalley? So my little garage in White Rock was converted into a food storage warehouse, and supplies were carried to the Whalley streets—every night, seven nights a week.

The Fraser Valley Real Estate Board's Blanket Drive provided hundreds of warm blankets. The Greater Vancouver Homebuilders' Association donated coats. The Sheraton Hotel provided surplus blankets. So much came in that we finally had to secure a small storage space in nearby Langley to store all the goods.

I continued in the cave, my cottage basement office, with the assistance of a practicum student from Trinity Western University for four hours a week. She was a blessing.

Glancing back over the year, the enemy had been relentless in trying to distract, discourage, and wear us down. He kept us chasing our tails as we tried to keep up with his constant harassment. But we fought back with love, persistence, patience, long-suffering, and endurance ... and some assistance from our earthly angels. The "Whalley

Israelites" had found a home. "Consider it pure joy, my brothers and sisters, whenever you face trials of many kinds, because you know that the testing of your faith produces perseverance. Let perseverance finish its work so that you may be mature and complete, not lacking anything" (James 1:2-5 NIV).

By God's grace we had made it through another year. Through the trials and tribulations, God was teaching us about trust and faith.

And yes, He was right.

It was pure joy.

DISCUSSION QUESTIONS

1. **Do you believe in angels?**
   - Why?
   - Is believing in angels biblical?

2. **Who are the angels in your life?**
   - What is the story?

3. **Do you believe God is faithful to you?**
   - What does the Bible say about His faithfulness? What are His promises?
   - When you are wandering in your own wilderness how do you lean into your faith?
   - How does that comfort you?
   - What does it mean to you to have someone you can count on?
   - Are you prepared to bring your fears, worries and unsolvable problems to God?

4. **Have you experienced 'pure joy'?**
   - Where does it come from?

Gentle Shepherd Church, 2004.

Mac's "mountain of food" located in her home garage in White Rock, 2005.

Bentley Field, 2005.

NightShift's clothing truck, 2005.

NightShift's outreach truck and food trailer on 135 Street, 2006.

Serving on 107 Avenue, Surrey.

Prayers are always available. *Photo courtesy of Chris Loh.*

Volunteers at work at NightShift's first home in 2006.

Exterior of NighShift's first home base location. *Photo courtesy of Chris Loh.*

NightShift's Clothing Ministry.

Saturday Nightlife Meetings were held at the 135 Street location in order to connect with God and one another.

Mac and Deni.

Soul food for Surrey's hungry. *Photo courtesy of Chris Loh.*

The Care Centre, NightShift Street Ministries, Sisters Thrift Boutique and RagTime now share a location at 10635 King George Boulevard, Surrey.

NightShift's offices. *Photo courtesy of Brian Hawkes.*

Team Leaders Meetings are held the third Wednesday of every month. *Photo courtesy of Ingrid Roeske Good.*

Chapter 15

CHANGES

O NE LAST EVENT of 2005 made an extraordinary change in our lives and the lives of the homeless on the streets of Whalley. On November 19, Dianne Watts, a former City of Surrey Councillor, was elected Mayor of Surrey.

She ran as an independent candidate and defeated the incumbent, Doug McCallum. She had campaigned on the theme that "a culture of control and conflict had developed at city hall" under the McCallum regime. She had that right. She promised "better cooperation between the provincial and city governments to bring more social services into Surrey to deal with homelessness, drug use, and crime" (Wikipedia). She won in a landslide.

Oh, happy day! Thank God. Happy dance. The moment she sat in that mayor's chair, the opposition backed off NightShift. Coincidental? No, I'd say, God looks after His kids.

Then it was Christmas. A week full of street events, worship, gifts, stockings, and treats—not to forget buckets of love. God was good.

We still had one last hurdle to jump. There was still that wee problem of a business license. You may recall the bylaw that prohibited not-for-profits from conducting community services. We still needed the mandatory paperwork and City Council's approval before a business license could be issued.

Mayor Watts was at the 2006 Winter Games in Torino, Italy, in February 2006. I emailed her that we had finally found a location for a new home, asking whether this location could be a possibility for us. In other words, if we can have this as a home, can we now secure a business license? We had been in the community for two years. Our noses were clean. Would this be a good time now? To my delight, the mayor answered immediately—from Torino! The answer was yes. What a woman. And to whom do you think she copied her email and directed my attention? None other than my old friend, John Sherstone.

Apparently the old Community Impact Statement requirement had left City Hall with the former mayor. It was now replaced with a Good Neighbour Agreement, which I totally supported. It remains in place today. After several months of back-and-forth meetings, we finished the paperwork, signed the documents, and hallelujah, we had our business license.

Well, God had always told me to expect miracles!

Gratefully, we moved into our new home, steps away from where we operated our nightly outreach service. It was the perfect location. There was enough room for an administration office, kitchen, and warehouse space. The only problem? We had no money. No damage deposit. No guarantee we could pay the monthly rent of $1,300. Scary. Talk about a faith walk. Trusting God for provisions, we nevertheless stepped forward as God opened the door. We successfully negotiated the space with no damage deposit and prayed the finances would come in time for the first month's rent. Of course it did. And it kept coming. Those were cliff-hanging times for sure. And if I'm perfectly honest, it hasn't changed much. We're still walking in faith every month, trusting God that He'll provide. Not maybe for our wants, mind you, but always for our needs. And He does, without fail. It keeps us on our knees.

Not only did He give us our business license, He also brought in the hands, feet, and hearts in amazing ways. It was almost like the famous quote from the 1989 movie, Field of Dreams, " If you build it, they will come." It was the busiest, dustiest time of my life. And the most exhausting.

There were moments I wasn't sure I was going to make it through another day.

I was beginning to feel the effects of burnout. Two of our original board members left NightShift to follow other paths. I was the only original board member remaining from our humble beginnings in 2004. Carrying much of the workload myself, especially in the area of administration, was too much for one person. I was still working from my White Rock basement office, travelling back and forth to Whalley several times a day.

My days went from "over-the-moon" excitement to "down-in-the-dumps" despair. I was tired. There were days—many in fact—that I'd call out to God, "Why me? This is too much. I don't know what I'm doing!"

God would answer, "I know you don't. But I do. I'll lead. You just take the step and follow Me."

So I did. One step at a time—one day at a time. I think God tricked me with that one-step-at-a-time thing of His. If I had known what I know now, would I have taken the next step? What do you think? You're right! Absolutely. In a heartbeat!

God continued to also bless us in other areas. We added to our volunteer numbers daily. Churches continued to join our teams. People flocked to information sessions. They heard the call, "Become part of the miracle in Whalley."

God had heard my plea for a Joshua—or in this case a Joshuaette. One of the board members came into our forever-under-renovation space and handed me two cheques for four hundred dollars.

"Go hire yourself an assistant," he said proudly.

To myself I said, "Are you crazy?" Where was I going to find someone willing to work for eight hundred dollars? That was it? No promise of more to come. But I pounced on it. Didn't God multiply bread and fish (John 6:1-15)?

This board member recommended two candidates. Our offices were a catastrophe. Our space looked like a bomb had gone off. The boardroom table couldn't be seen for boxes and stuff. I shoved a few to the side, clearing a space for our meeting.

The first interview went well. She was smart. Fast thinker. Strong. I casually mentioned that our vacuum cleaner needed an overhaul. She left with it in her hands. Hmm. A maybe.

The second one walked in, looked around, and started to shake. Okay, I'm exaggerating. She was very sweet. Way too sweet for our chaos. We were finishing our interview an hour later when Number One Candidate walked through the door carrying the Hoover, plunked it down, dusted off her hands and said, "It's fixed." Smiling over her shoulder, she walked out the door.

I hired her. On the spot! Carmen and me. A tag team made in heaven! Poor girl, she didn't really know what she was getting into. Eight hundred dollars didn't get us far. Talk about faith. She was willing to work until the funds appeared. They did four months later. I will be forever grateful to her for her courage, faith, and tenacity. She has what it takes to serve in this ministry. She has guts. She's a true NightShifter.

We went to work. And I mean work. We whipped that space into shape with the help of volunteers, builders, tradespeople, suppliers, and lots of prayers; our extensive renovation was done in about four months' time. No budget. A labour of love. We have tons of fond memories from that time. A multitude of miracle stories to tell!

What I remember most from the weeks and months that followed was how crazy busy I was again. The word was out. People were saying good things. There was a hunger for information about what we were doing on the street. People were hungry for God.

NightShift, the little organic, grassroots ministry, was coming into its own. That spring, I had scheduled presentations about the NightShift story to more than a dozen churches and schools. Did I mention that I was almost as

terrified of speaking in public as I was when I first came
to Whalley?

I was about to be tested again.

Public speaking has never been my gift. Remember, I'm
not a preacher. I would prepare for days and days about what
I wanted to say. I'd have my notes ready. I'd pretend I knew
what I was doing. But sitting alone in the front pew, waiting
for my time to step up to the microphone, I trembled.

I'd rather jump off a bridge than speak in front of people.
It literally made me sick to my stomach. Nine out of ten
times, before it was my turn to speak, I felt the Holy Spirit
descend upon me, overwhelming me, and I would weep.
And I mean weep—in front of the entire church.

I was sure people were gawking at me, wondering who
this basket case was. The thought of going up there hor-
rified me. By the time I stepped up on the platform, I was
emotionally drained. My nose was running, my eyes were
bloodshot and swollen, and my mascara was running down
my face. Nice. The person having the nervous breakdown
was representing NightShift.

Once in front of the microphone, I had forgotten what
I was going to say. Talk about humbling. When I could
no longer see my notes through my tears, I opened my
mouth and that's when God showed up. I spoke what He
downloaded. And don't ask me what I said after I finished.
I had no recollection. Ever. How nerve-wracking was that?

But I had a story to tell: God's story, about His little street ministry in Whalley.

I love to tell stories. So we made a good team.

God pointed me to Moses' story in Exodus. I felt a lot like Moses. Stutterer. Stumbling over my words. An ineffective communicator and definitely not a public speaker, right?

> Moses said to the LORD, "Pardon your servant, Lord. I have never been eloquent, neither in the past nor since you have spoken to your servant. I am slow of speech and tongue." The LORD said to him, "Who gave human beings their mouths? Who makes them deaf or mute? Who gives them sight or makes them blind? Is it not I, the LORD? Now go; I will help you speak and will teach you what to say."
>
> —Exodus 4:10-12 NIV

Humbling, but I learned to trust God in this area too. He put His words in my mouth. He has never failed me. I'm sure you've heard this phrase before, "God does not call the equipped. He equips the called."

Amen to that.

DISCUSSION QUESTIONS

1. How do you feel about change?
- Are you ready for change to shift your life?
- What does it mean to have the courage to do the work without knowing if the results will come?
- Do you ever wonder, "Why me? This is too much", or "I don't know what I am doing!"
- Do you ask God those questions? How does He respond?

2. When you are tired, overwhelmed, confused—do you call out to God?
- Does He answer you?
- Do you find comfort?
- What is your next step in turning to God to guide you?

3. What are your spiritual gifts?
- What is God's story that He tells through you?
- How has God equipped you for your journey?

Chapter 16

VISION

THE VISION HAD been born some Christmases before at the Ukrainian Orthodox Church when a homeless man eating a turkey dinner slumped forward in his chair and his face dropped into the plate. I cleaned his face, a face covered in sores, and the embryo was planted in my heart. It hadn't lain dormant. It proved to be the living, breathing heartbeat of the ministry. But there was more.

Slowly, God's idea developed into a seed pollinated by the Holy Spirit over a two-year period. "Before a seed there comes the thought of the bloom" (E. B. White, 1899-1985). God had been preparing the soil, germinating the seed, into reality. The seed of His vision was making its appearance out of darkness into the light.

The people we loved on the street weren't perfect. Their lives were messy. Over time, we developed close relationships, a level of trust earned only from our constant presence on the street. What was becoming increasingly difficult for us to accept was that we could only help so much.

We were experiencing enormous difficulty in placing people under the influence of alcohol or drugs or struggling with mental health issues, or both, into appropriate recovery facilities. High barrier intake procedures (such as forty-eight hours of abstinence or longer), long waiting lists, and a lack of reputable recovery options made placement almost impossible. More often than not, recovery facilities did not utilize the services of outreach workers like NightShift to connect directly and consistently with people in the midst of their addictions or living on the street. This became a huge barrier. People were slipping through the cracks.

When one of our street friends finally musters up the courage to come forward genuinely wanting help, too often it is an opportunity lost. They are turned away. Time and time again. There are crucial gaps between frontline outreach and sustained recovery that prove deadly. Sadly, many have died while seeking recovery.

Sheri

Do you recall Sheri? The young woman, age thirty-three, whom I prayed over the first week at the Gentle Shepherd? Here's a short excerpt from a Spring 2004 update. I wrote about the girl who had captivated my heart:

> Sheri's street partner has died of an overdose. She awoke to find him dead lying beside her. One can only imagine her trauma. Heartbroken, and alone, she continued her relationship with heroin. The deadly addiction set in.

She now works the street in the area she grew up in. The stores she once shopped in as a girl are now forbidden to her. She is humiliated, embarrassed and ashamed. Her three children live with her mother. The cry of her heart is to have them back. She desperately misses them and wishes she could be there for them. But her addiction doesn't allow this. Its deadly grip controls her life. Her health continues to worsen. We fear for her life.

Sheri went underground. Two years later, still struggling with her addiction, she appeared again. She walked up to me on the street one night.

"Mac, I need help," she sobbed. "Please save me. I want my life back."

I'd been praying for Sheri for two years. This time she genuinely wanted help. My help. She promised to call me the next day. Part of me thought she might not. There's just a sliver of opportunity to rescue people with addictions when they cry out, "Help me." They reach out their hand, only to have it tugged back by the next hit of the drug. The enemy snarls, "How dare you think you can get away?" They slip away in the dark, back to their poisonous addiction and the demons assigned to kill them. But Sheri did call me the next morning. And the next. Every morning for a week. Each time, her voice was more urgent.

I can't tell you how many recovery homes were contacted. I was desperate to find a place but not one would take her. The reasons were various, but mostly it was because she hadn't detoxed for a few days. Remember, I don't take no for an answer but this time, I was forced to admit there wasn't a place for Sheri.

This was another turning point for me.

I had let Sheri down. Big time. I heard it in her voice the next time she called. She was crushed. I was crushed. I had worked hard to develop a trusting relationship with her, only to have it extinguished, perhaps forever. She slipped away. Angry. Disappointed. I didn't hear from her again. Until one year later.

God has wired my mind as a visual learner. So knowing this, He began to download a picture in my spirit. I'm a doodler, so I scribbled out a rough map through my devotional times with Him. The only analogy or explanation I can compare this process to is this: do you remember the old analog television sets that displayed a snowy screen until the channel kicked in? Slowly the picture unfolded as the reception cleared. I know I'm showing my age here, but that's what it looked like in my spirit. I'd get a waif of an idea, a snowy-out-there-kind-of-idea and slowly, over time, it would start to take shape.

God called the seed forth that He had been fertilizing in my spirit. He breathed on the dream that He had pressed into my heart in the early days of the ministry. The dream, so huge, so unattainable, so beyond reach, that my words couldn't describe it. After Sheri's last phone call, the idea quickly took form. The antenna kicked in. The snowy reception cleared. I had the image.

I knew more had to be done to prevent people from slipping through the cracks—more than serving a hot meal and providing clothing and emergency shelter. "I was hungry and you fed me" (Matt. 25:40 NIV).

What would it look like if all stages of recovery were available within one organization? Could we provide such a service that would catch the Sheri's of our city, rescue them, and bring them through short-term stabilization (detox) when they were ready to fight for their lives? What would it look like if we had our own long-term recovery offering training for reintegration, including counselling, life and work skill programs, education and employment placement, and reintegration mentorship?

To accomplish this, we needed to establish a continuum of support and care to help transition our street friends from their addictions and street environment through to successful reintegration as contributing members of the community. NightShift's mission is to love unconditionally and to help people find hope and purpose. Was this what God wanted us to do? Offer more than soup and emergency shelter? As the months flew by, He continued to cultivate, fertilize, and nourish the idea with His living water. The sprout began to appear.

Isaiah 61 talks about setting captives free, binding up broken hearts, and providing beauty for ashes.

> The Spirit of the Sovereign LORD is on me, because the LORD has anointed me to proclaim good news to the poor. He has sent me to bind up the broken-hearted, to proclaim freedom for the captives and release from darkness for the prisoners, to proclaim the year of the LORD's favour and the day of vengeance of our God, to comfort all who mourn, and provide for those who grieve in Zion, to bestow on them a crown of beauty instead of

ashes, the oil of joy instead of mourning, and a garment of praise instead of a spirit of despair....

—Isaiah 61:1-3 ESV

Isaiah 61 became the foundational scripture for NightShift's Care Vision. The Vision began to grow with a focus on prayer and counselling to help people discover the reasons behind their pain and brokenness. It was the same process that God used to set me free. God doesn't waste pain. He's used all of my pain and anguish for His glory. "Blessed be the God and Father of our Lord Jesus Christ, the Father of mercies and God of all comfort, who comforts us in all our affliction so that we will be able to comfort those who are in any affliction with the comfort with which we ourselves are comforted" (2 Cor. 1:3-4 ESV).

He wanted those perishing on the street to know His comfort, His saving grace, His redeeming love. "… They will be called oaks of righteousness, a planting of the LORD for the display of his splendour … Instead of your shame you will receive a double portion, and instead of disgrace you will rejoice in your inheritance. And so you will inherit a double portion in your land, and everlasting joy will be yours" (Isa. 61:3, 7 NIV).

The homeless are suffering and perishing on our streets every day. Some escape; more often than not, they don't. It's not by choice. A life of pain has driven them there. Dr. Michael Krausz, lead researcher for The Centre for Health Evaluation and Outcome Services (CHEOS) at the University of British Columbia and St. Paul's Hospital, commented on their survey of 500 chronically homeless people in three B.C. communities:

A higher-than-expected level of childhood trauma with 80 percent of participants suffering significant trauma, abuse, violence, or emotional neglect as children. Most of the study participants have experienced more than one type of maltreatment, experiences that have devastating lasting impact, including moderate to high risk of suicide. Many also suffered severe mental health challenges such as schizophrenia, mood disorders, and fetal alcohol syndrome.

I'm curious. At whose hands did they experience trauma, violence, abuse, or emotional neglect? Who's responsible? I'll step out on a limb and say, "We are." And what are we doing about it?

This was life and death. God's compassion compelled me to do something to help the plight of those dying right in front of my eyes. The "driving force" term that had been used to describe me by several newspapers, slid into overdrive. The need is now.

Sheri lost the fight on Christmas 2007—a young life terminated by addiction and cancer. She called me one night from the hospital, a few days before she died. By then, Sheri had accepted Jesus as her Lord and Saviour. She knew she was going to heaven. But that didn't take away the years of pain and heartache. It didn't erase the guilt of leaving three children behind without a mother. It didn't remove the blanket of shame that remained tightly entwined about her.

For the rest of my life, I will hear the agony of her wailing, her soul crying out for a life lost.

Before she went to be with Jesus, I had told Sheri about a place. A place I dreamed about. Where women and men could run to from the deadly grip of addictions. Cottages. A village, a haven of safety and love. A place where people could escape the horror and abuse of the street. A place to breathe, heal, and recover from the cruel blows of life. Sheri knew one day that dream would come true. I remember the sparkle in her eyes and the sweet smile that slowly spread across her beautiful face—the day I told her she was the inspiration behind the cottages.

If we'd had a cottage for her on the day she cried out for help, maybe her life would have turned out differently. Only God knows that. Sheri stepped into eternal life with Jesus, knowing that one day, back here on earth, there would be a cottage door with her name on it.

God doesn't waste pain.

DISCUSSION QUESTIONS

1. **Do you believe 'we are responsible'?**
   - Why? Why not?
   - If we are how can we help?

2. **How has pain driven you to do something you regret?**
   - How has trauma, abuse, violence or emotional neglect impacted you?
   - How did you grow and learn from it?
   - How does it still bind you?
   - Has prayer and counselling ever helped you understand and move beyond pain and anguish?
   - How have you experienced God's grace and comfort?

3. **Have you reached a turning point?**
   - Have you come to it yet?

4. **Do you have a vision for your life?**
   - What is your big dream?
   - What is God preparing for you to do?
   - What will be the contribution of your life?

Chapter 17

ONE LIFE

S HERI'S DEATH BROUGHT me a heightened sense
of awareness of the value of human life. I struggled
with the question of what one life is worth.

What's your life worth? What about your children's
lives? Your family's? Your best friend's? My life? The lives
that have been touched by this story?

We applaud someone for saving another person—from
drowning, for example. We consider rescuers heroes. Medals.
Media attention. Celebrations. I don't mean to minimize
heroic acts, for they definitely are a demonstration of our
collective humanity, but conversely I don't hear the accolade
given to someone who has saved a homeless person's life
from starvation, hypothermia, or addictions. Aren't they
drowning too?

What about the rescuer who unselfishly invests money
into saving someone's life?

People often like to invest in palatable charities. Animal shelters, sick children, cancer ... all exceptionally worthwhile charities. But what about the people living on our streets? The ones who are not pretty to look at. The ones struggling with mental illness, alcohol and drug addiction. The homeless. They're not that appealing, are they? Ask me. At one point in my life, I didn't want to touch one. Why? Because many of us still carry the stigmas about the lepers in modern society.

"Get a job." "You're a bum." Are they not worthwhile too? Thankfully, God has changed my heart dramatically and has shifted my thinking in the trenches.

What is one life worth, I wondered—in hard cash dollars?

I know that's not a particularly Christian point of view, but bear with me. I have potential contributors to convince. Just as if I were running a company, the people who donate to NightShift are like investors, and investors want to know what's the return on their investment, the ROI.

According to Wikipedia,

In finance, rate of return (ROR), also known as (ROI), is the ration of money gained or lost (whether realized or unrealized) on an investment relative to the amount of money invested. Shrewd investors use these terms to decide if they should invest in a new project or business. They compare the return of an investment to all other available options, taking the risk-free rate of return, inflation, and liquidity into consideration.

So what kind of costs are we talking about? What's the cost of one life? Measured by how much the government spends to keep one person alive and well, the per capita cost of health care in Canada is $3,678 per year (U.S. dollars, compared to $6,714 in the USA). In Canada, the government subsidizes about 70 percent of that, according to the Organization for Economic Co-operation and Development (OECD). So keeping alive one average Canadian costs about $2,575 annually. Meanwhile, cost of keeping a man incarcerated in federal prison in Canada for one year is $113,974 according to the Toronto Sun (2012). Add to that, each year the Province of British Columbia spends over $294 million for families and persons in need, according to the B.C. 2012 budget. And the costs to taxpayers of shelters, hospitals, ambulances, and paramedic services for the homeless—none of which are paid for by Medicare—are staggering, to say the least.

In strictly financial terms, it's fair to summarize that for you and me, in sickness and health—just as for the prisoners and the paupers—Canada's taxpayers already invest a lot of money in us. Collectively as Canadians, the dollar value we place on a human life is substantial. We perceive life as valuable. (Presumably, in some parts of our planet that is not the case. We should be grateful we are here.)

Now to rescue this valuable commodity from homelessness and, in many cases, drug addiction, investors in my business want to know how quickly they can expect results. What's the turnaround time? How many people did you get off the street, into detox, into recovery, into a job, into a meaningful life?

Some expect an immediate return on their investment—as if it were real estate speculation or a stock market play—but most investors know it doesn't work that way. Take retirement savings plans, for example. How many times have we heard, "Don't panic and pull your funds out in a fluctuating market. Leave them to mature. Over time, you'll reap the benefits of the extraordinary power of compound interest."

I think we can apply the same principle here. Yes, I'm a "Let's-wrap-it-up-in-two-weeks" kind of girl myself. I want change—*fast*—especially in my life, but I've learned the hard way that change takes time. It's a journey, often a marathon, to reach the final destination. I've rarely been blessed with "a quick around the block" success in achieving something worthwhile. Have you? It takes commitment, guts, and hard work.

It takes time for my street friends too. An ultra-marathon! And they're coming from way behind. A friend once said, "NightShift is not a MacDonald's drive-through. We're not a quick, fast-food remedy for change." Absolutely. "If you're expecting instant change," my friend added, "you're in for a big disappointment. Are you in for the long or short haul?"

So how do I respond to the hard questions of some NightShift financial supporters who are struggling with the questions:

"How many people does NightShift save from the street?"

"How many go into recovery and transition into a changed life?"

"What's the ministry's success rate?"

"What's the rate of return on my investment?"

I understand these questions. I asked the same questions ten years ago. I looked to the natural. Not to the spiritual. I placed a price tag on things.

What's a life worth that is perishing on the streets of our cities? Life and death. Eternal life. What's that worth?

In the New Testament, Jesus tells a story about how much one life is worth to God: The Parable of The Lost Sheep. A shepherd had one hundred sheep and lost one of them. He left the ninety-nine and went looking for the one until he found it. "'… Rejoice with me; I have found my lost sheep.' I tell you that in the same way there will be more rejoicing in heaven over one sinner who repents than over ninety-nine righteous persons who do not need to repent" (Luke 15:4-7 NIV).

If one person repents and turns his or her life around, it's worth more than ninety-nine of us who have already repented. The Shepherd is relentlessly persistent. He keeps looking and won't give up "until He finds it." What's one life worth to the Shepherd?

Remember Crissy, the homeless woman and drug addict, who changed her life and became part of NightShift's outreach—now helping others off the street and into new rewarding lives? What's the ripple effect of her life? What's the effect of the expanding ripples of love spreading across pain and suffering, touching and transforming lives? How many others are radically affected because she got her life back? Her daughters? Her family? Her friends on the street who caught a glimmer of hope, inspired by her courage? What's that worth? How many lives are changed by the touch of one person? Can you place a dollar value on that?

Of course, there is no guarantee people's lives will change. There's no risk-free investment. But remember the Ultimate Broker is God. And the currency He works with is unconditional love. No expectations. No judgment. His guarantee is this: He will multiply our gifts in more ways than we could ever imagine. There will be a ripple effect that flows from our investment into another's life—whether it is an investment of our finances or that of our hearts.

The ultimate ROI? Pure joy. There's nothing that compares to it. That indescribable feeling that you get deep down in your belly when you've helped to make a difference in another's life, especially "the least of these." A big ear-to-ear grin thrill. You might not see the benefit today, tomorrow, or even in your lifetime. No one else may see what you sow. But God sees it. The rewards are incomparable. "Do not be deceived: God cannot be mocked. A man reaps what he sows. Whoever sows to please their flesh, from the flesh will reap destruction; whoever sows to please the Spirit, from the Spirit will reap eternal life. Let us not become weary in doing good, for in the proper time we will reap a harvest if we do not give up" (Gal. 6:7-9 ESV).

Maybe we won't know until we reach heaven. Imagine when we get there how awesome will that be? To meet the people God has used—that includes you and me—who led them to Jesus and eternal life. That'll be one hallelujah party!

What's one life worth? Well, God won't give up looking—nor will we—until He has the lost ones safely tucked in his arms! That's your ROI. And it's the best investment you can make. Guaranteed.

What about the cost when we lose one? The one who doesn't make it? It happens every day.

As I write this, my heart is heavy. I'm remembering. In the second year of the ministry, I received a phone call from a young woman who wanted to "give back." She said her name was Brooke. There was something about her voice that tugged on my spirit. In spite of my busyness, I agreed to meet her for coffee at a local restaurant.

I saw at once there was something different about her. Mary's heart. A natural beauty. She was hesitant. Shy. Humble. Quiet spirit. Soft-spoken. Curiously, she couldn't bring her eyes to look into mine. Not for a second. For the entire conversation, she spoke looking down at the table. Pain. Shame. She shared a bit of her story. It's not mine to tell but I know she would be okay with me telling you that she battled with addictions. Crystal methadone was her poison. It had stolen her life for many years. She was passionate about sharing her story with others—in an effort to free them from the enemy's deadly net.

One Sunday afternoon, she came to visit with her three-year-old daughter, Cora, a bundle of sweetness. Vivacious! We spent the afternoon together with my two golden retrievers, and as Brooke and her daughter ascended the steps to leave, Cora looked over her shoulder and said, "Don't forget to dream about me!" in the sweetest sing-song voice ever! I was captivated.

It was obvious that Brooke adored Cora. She took motherhood seriously. She had a passion for Jesus, and so did her daughter. Cora attended a Christian school. Brooke graduated from Bible school and volunteered with NightShift. And over time, her soft eyes rose slowly to look lovingly into mine. The calling on her life was evident to all of us. Everyone loved her. Her heart's desire was to work in a recovery home, helping women like her to stay clean. We often talked about her dream and the day she would become a full-time counsellor in one of our recovery cottages. She was a godly woman of courage and strength. She was blossoming into becoming the woman that God had called her to be. She had made it. Escaped the deadly grip of crystal meth—against all odds. I was immensely proud of her. So was Brooke's mother. She wrote:

I am the mother of a twenty-three-year-old daughter whose drug of choice was "crystal meth."

This is a highly addictive drug and the "high" can last twenty-four to forty-eight hours. This deadly drug can be made quite easily and is very inexpensive to purchase. It contains such things as lye, ether, and even drain cleaner. The people selling this drug, of course, do not tell them this. They are only wanting to get rich at the expense of their sick and innocent victims.

I began to notice drastic changes. She became very paranoid, believing people were following her. She believed her boyfriend had planted a hearing device inside her head and she started hearing voices. These voices would torment her day and night even when she wasn't "high." She began to see things that were not there and she pleaded with me to take her to the doctor's to have this device removed. She began to cut at herself saying the physical pain was more bearable than the mental pain. The more I explained it was the drugs she was doing, the more paranoid she became, believing that there was a conspiracy against her. At one point she actually believed I had hired a hit man to have her killed.

We had her committed to the psychiatric ward on several occasions but they would only sedate her until she became somewhat stable and then release her. Eventually she started to show signs of schizophrenia and they placed her on anti-psychotic medication and sent her to Riverview Hospital.

I have now sent my daughter to a safe place hundreds of miles from here and she is finally getting the help she needs to heal. Crystal meth does a lot of damage to people who use it and the long-term effects are not yet fully known. It is killing our children and destroying our families.

As a concerned mother I would ask that you continue to inform our kids out there of how deadly this drug really is and let them know there is help out there through Mental Health, Addiction Services and also their local church ... before it's too late.

Brooke and I connected every Christmas for six years—except one. That last Christmas, I received a phone call unexpectedly from Brooke's mother. I could feel her grief across the miles.

"She's gone," I heard her mother say.

Brooke was found dead in a motel a few blocks away from NightShift's offices. Alone. Suspected overdose. I was sickened and saddened. This shouldn't have happened. Not Brooke! She had made it. She had fought the good fight. Seven years! Then I got mad. Really mad! At the enemy of her soul, who viciously and relentlessly tormented and condemned her. I was even more determined to see our recovery cottages become a reality.

I spoke at Brooke's funeral. The place was packed. As I looked out over the crowd, my eyes rested on a beautiful young girl sitting in the front pew. Cora. I hadn't seen her for a number of years. My heart broke for this child. With difficulty, I read from the pages of Brooke's purpose statement that she had written at Bible school:

What will be the centre of my life? "Getting to know and become more and more like my friend and Saviour."

What will be the character of my life? "My purpose is to love God and people."

What will my contribution of my life? "My purpose is to serve wherever I am needed."

What will be the communication of my life? "My purpose will be to lead people to Jesus Christ by speaking the truth in love and exhibiting His supernatural power to heal and set people free."

Brooke achieved all these purposes that God placed in her heart. She had compassion for the broken and a passion to set captives free. We witnessed that time and time again when she was seen earnestly talking to someone on the street. It was impossible to contain her. How many lives had been touched by Brooke's life? How many have heard the good news? How many came to Jesus? Countless.

What is one life worth?

Brooke's name, like Sheri's, will be on one of our cottage doors. I only wish she were here with us to see my dream become a reality. It was her dream too.

The ripple effect? Cora and I have become close friends. I see her every month. She is pure joy! A blessing. We talk about her mother a lot. Cora's loss. Her grief. She knows God has a calling on her life. She knows pain, and she wants to help others in pain—just like her mother did.

Recently, Cora presented me with a beautiful card and a charming gift—a handmade soft blue knitted coaster for my coffee mug. Created by her own hands and heart. How precious is that? Every stitch was a stitch of love. Her labour of love, for me. I'll cherish it forever. What's the ripple effect? Her card touched me deeply.

"Mac, thank you for being my counsellor," she had written. "Here is a $100 cheque for you. Please put it towards the Care Village. I know my Mom would have wanted me to. I love you, Cora."

Yes, sweet Cora, your Mom would want you to do this. You have honoured her memory. Brooke is smiling proudly! God doesn't waste pain.

This gift was given to Cora as a Christmas present. That's a lot of money for a ten-year-old. She unselfishly gave it all to help others like her mother. Her gift was the very first seed sown for the Care Village. I have a feeling that God will multiply this humble seed a thousandfold.

Every time Cora leaves my office, she turns and looks back at me with sparkling eyes and a playful smile, and sings, "Don't forget to dream about me."

What is one life worth?

DISCUSSION QUESTIONS

1. **How does the world show that we value human life?**
   - How does it show that we don't?
   - What does that say about our society?
   - Why do we care more for people with cancer or sick children or abused animals than we do for people who are struggling with poverty, homelessness, addictions or mental health challenges?
   - What can we do to show people who are homeless, drug addicted or mentally ill that we value their life?

2. **What effect do you think your life has had on others?**
   - Is your life a ripple?
   - How many lives are changed by the touch of one person?
   - Describe one person who has made a shift in their lives and inspired you?
   - Why does it inspire you?

3. **What areas of your life need God's healing touch?**
   - Have you witnessed this in your life, in the lives of others?

Chapter 18

VISION LEAKS

I N RESPONSE TO the deaths of Brooke and Sheri—and because I knew the enemy lurking in our streets—I was dreaming a new, fuller vision of NightShift. I saw outreach programs expand to include a mobile bus unit offering mobile counselling, prayer ministry, street-level nursing, and basic dental services. A counselling centre offering licensed counselling services with sliding fees so no one would be turned away because of lack of money. And our own recovery program with short-term stabilization, long-term care, and after-care reintegration homes.

It was a big but interrelated program to provide a way out from the cruel life on the streets and a way back into a life with meaning. My doodling started to take on the form of a six-phased plan that God would unfold over the next five years. I was anxious to get started.

As I mentioned, my tendency is to want to wrap things up in two weeks. Get on with it! Waiting is very difficult for me, and people were dying. But God had a plan. In His timing. In His impeccable timing!

So I waited until He would open the door and beckon us through. Then one morning, an angel left this message. I never did discover who taped the note to the laptop on my desk.

"Be still," it read. "Watch, listen, and discern. There is a temporary divine silence around you, and you must wait for My direction. Rest in My presence and be rejuvenated as you wait for My leading. Cease striving and refuse the temptation to get caught up in the rush and competition that the world produces. Be strong but silent, says the Lord."

Yes, the note referred to "Wait for the Lord; be strong and take heart (be encouraged) and wait for the Lord" (Ps. 27:14 NIV).

This spoke to my heart. A temporary divine silence was around me. Wait for His direction. Rest and wait for His leading. And what did I do? I went searching for the meaning of *wait*. I was frustrated waiting. I needed to hear from God.

I read. I prayed. He revealed a greater depth. I sensed it meant more than being "still." More than spending quality time with Him. More than waiting expectantly for something to happen. Hmm.

So I'm leaning in for revelation. Joyce Meyer spoke about *wait* in her *Mount Up with Wings as Eagles* DVD. She compared "wait" to "a hair strand that we braid, so closely knit together, it's hard to tell one strand from the other." I instantly thought of Father, Son, and the Holy Spirit.

But wait! Have patience. There's more. "He gives strength to the weary and increases the power of the weak. Even youths grow tired and weary, and young men stumble and fall; but those who hope in the Lord will renew their strength. They will soar on wings like eagles; they will run and not grow weary, they will walk and not be faint" (Isa. 40:29–31 NIV).

I found something rather amazing. Many, many years ago, I had written in the margin of my Bible, "Surrender, admit my weakness, stop fainting. Take your single strand of weakness and wrap it around the strong strand of God. Wait and I'll gain God's perspective on my situation." Whew, was God showing me something or what?

I was struggling with loneliness, exhaustion, anxiety, and feeling overwhelmed. My plate was full. We were short of finances again, stretched with not enough hands. "God, can you hurry? I need your help!" So once again, I surrendered to Papa, admitted my weakness, and asked for His forgiveness for relying on my own strength, not His. My eyes rested on, "You are my servant, I have chosen you and have not rejected you. So do not fear, for I am with you; do not be dismayed, for I am your God. I will strengthen you and help you; I will uphold you with my righteous right hand" (Isa. 41:9-10 NIV).

And more revelation! Listen to what I learned about the meaning of *wait*.

In Hebrew, the sense of waiting on the Lord is called *qavah*. *Qavah* means: to bind together like a twisted rope, to look patiently, and to hope eagerly. Waiting, entwined with patience and hope. Be patient. Don't quit. Have hope. Don't doubt. Wait. He'll move in His time. He revealed that if I stop hoping, I stop waiting. If I stop being patient, I'll stop waiting.

Isn't it interesting how this intertwines, how it comes together in an amazing way? I love it! So I patiently waited and hoped expectantly.

But while I waited patiently, I confess I grew increasingly discouraged with our board involvement. We needed a strong team and enough finances to make the Care Vision happen. It was beyond Carmen and me. The vision was constantly threatened by board instability and lack of unity as members came and went as the ministry grew. Time and time again, I appealed for their help with the challenging task of raising funds while my infamous "Things to Do" list grew in mega portions. Often my appeals fell on deaf ears.

Gathering busy board members together, whose lives are consumed with the present challenges of daily living—family and business—on a regular basis was and continues to be very challenging, especially in maintaining their commitment and passion about the Care Vision. Pastor Andy Stanley, author of *Making Vision Stick*, wisely states, "The urgent and legitimate needs of today erase our commitment to the what could be of tomorrow." Too frequently, I witnessed important ministry decisions being made through our natural eyes, not spiritual. God calls us to walk in faith and to use our "spiritual" eyes and not rely on what is seen in the natural. "Now faith is being sure of what we hope for and certain of what we do not see" (Heb. 11:1 NIV).

In story after story, the Bible recounts how God's people didn't believe His promises and complained when things didn't look, in the natural, favourable. In fact, God, even though merciful, destroyed His people for their unbelief. It was like a poison to Him. For example, take Moses and the Israelites who couldn't enter the land of milk and honey that God promised them—because of unbelief. God told Moses to send out a representative from each of the twelve tribes in Israel to spy on the Promised Land. Upon their return, ten of the spies reported that had seen giants in the land, making it impossible for them to enter in.

In contrast to the giants, they saw themselves as grasshoppers. "… next to them we felt like grasshoppers, and that's what they felt too!" (Num. 13:33 NLT). Two of the ten spies believed God, "We should go up and take possession of the land, for we can surely do it" (Num. 13:30 NLT). "If the Lord is pleased with us, He will lead us into the land flowing with milk and honey … the Lord is with us. Do not be afraid of them" (Num. 14:8, 9 NIV).

From the ministry's early beginnings, we were very concerned that future boards understood addiction and brokenness and walked by faith in following God's vision when making ministry Care Vision decisions. I was rapidly learning that not only did I need to have faith that God was with us, but I also had to believe it! "And without faith it is impossible to please God, because anyone who comes to him must believe that he exists and that he rewards those who earnestly seek him" (Heb. 11:6 NIV).

God was showing me that unbelief goes deeper than lack of faith. Unbelief means "unbelieving." It suggests we are calling God a liar. His Word is not true. The root of sin is unbelief. When I don't believe God, His Word, or His promises, I'm operating in the sin of unbelief.

So I asked myself continually, "Do I truly believe God for where He is leading us? Do I see giants—as a grasshopper would and as one of the ten spies, who didn't believe God's promises, did? Or am I one of the two scouts who doesn't view opposition as impossible and instead believes God for the possible? Where do our board members stand in their belief? Do they truly grasp the Care Vision and understand the direction God is leading the ministry?"

Stanley says, "Vision is about what could be and should be, but life is about right this minute. Vision doesn't stick; it doesn't have a natural adhesive. Instead, vision leaks. You've repeated the vision a hundred times. Then someone will ask a question that makes you think, *What happened? Didn't they hear what we've said over and over? Don't they know what this church [ministry] is all about?*" Oh, how I identified with this.

According to Stanley, "Your vision is the lifeblood of your organization." Encouraged, I read on, "As the keeper of the vision, there's a lot working against you. Actually, it's worse than that. Just about everything is working against you. Success. Failure. Time. Life. But if, in spite of all that, there's something in you that refuses to give up and settle for the status quo, you may very well be the person God will use to bring about change."

Amen to that!

But in truth, poisonous discouragement was my constant enemy during this time. I know this doesn't sound like much of a threatening spear. It was more subtle but was still very much a source of toxic distraction that attacked me on a regular basis. As I type these words today, I reflect upon an excerpt from my journal written during these times about courage, encouragement, and discouragement.

I awakened this morning with a single word—courage—in my thoughts. I don't normally wake up with a word resonating in my head, so my curiosity was aroused. How strange—especially when I'm not feeling courageous these days—in fact the exact opposite—struggling with where to go next with the ministry.

As I lay there looking up at the ceiling, my thoughts drifted to two other words that were derivatives of the word *courage*. It occurred to me that there might be a message for me—a connection between the words *courage*, *encourage*, and *discourage*—that God wanted to show me. I dismissed the thought as my day settled into its hectic routine, but the word kept "pinging" at the back of my head and wouldn't stop until I decided to do something about it. I went digging for the meanings. What I found was very interesting.

Courage means the ability to face danger, difficulty, uncertainty, or pain without being overcome by fear or being deflected from a chosen course of action.

Encourage means to give somebody hope, confidence, or courage—to urge somebody in a helpful way to do or be something.

Discourage means to prevent something from happening by making it more difficult or unpleasant—to try and stop somebody from doing something—to make somebody feel less motivated, confident, or optimistic.

There it was. I've been battling discouragement—to the exact words of the definition—less motivated, confident, and optimistic. I was beginning to second-guess myself, letting fear creep in—guilt and blame to poison my spirit. I was suddenly struck with the reality the enemy was "dissing" me! He had put a "dis" in front of God's encouragement. The turmoil in my life has been a subtle ploy of the enemy to discourage me and to prevent me from accomplishing the task that God has set out before me. His motive was to have me "give up."

So I asked God to encourage me today. It seems He had already answered my prayer upon my wakening, before I even asked. With His one word—courage! He wanted me to be courageous—to stand firm against danger, difficulty, uncertainty, or pain and not to be overcome by fear or deflected from the course of action He has called me to do. He wants me to hold my head high in spite of the pain.

I need to clarify something here. I know what scripture tells me about courage, encouragement, and discouragement. I can hear my faithful friends' words of encouragement to stand firm in spite of the difficulties. But I can assure you that nothing compares to the joy when the God of the universe comes down and speaks to me on my level in such a creative way. It gets my attention—oceans tremble, eagles soar, and mountains move.

Revelation! Truth! Victory! He is my Encourager. He is my only source of Courage.

So I mustered up my God-courage and gathered a group of businessmen together from my pre-ministry life and assembled an advisory committee that ran alongside the board. This committee generously provided funds to help pay the rent and a small salary. By October 2006, I was able to receive a regular income. Well, sort of regular. Some months, yes. Other months, not so. It depended on what came in the door. There were needs that had priority over my salary, and those came first. The career girl who had earned a six-figure income in her previous life was bringing home substantially less. But it was just enough to live on. God provided in other ways. I never lacked. Nor did NightShift.

I realized that if the board ceased to embrace the Care Vision, I couldn't blame them for not following. It was my responsibility to lead and continually cast the Vision to the board, staff, and volunteers so it wouldn't leak. I believe God nudged my heart to prepare the Vision—*visually*. My heart on paper.

I have a confession to make, a character defect. Sometimes I expect others to know what's rolling around in my head without ever explaining what I'm thinking. This isn't the army; it's very difficult to get everyone aligned without them knowing the big picture. Now it was time to present the vision, coloured on a piece of poster board, for all to see.

I have to be honest. It was a bit unnerving. What if they didn't understand? What if they didn't get it, God? There wasn't another model out there that I could find that proved this was doable. There were pieces of it, but none that completed the continuum of care recovery process that I believed God wanted us to do. So in faith, once again, I stepped out in obedience. He did the rest. I'm not a graphic designer but with the Holy Spirit, my Guide and Counsellor, we organized an image board to present the God-vision to the board for approval.

It's amazing how much vision leaks. I've talked about this idea for years, but it wasn't until it was visual that people started to catch it. I'm told I'm a visionary, a big-picture thinker, which I guess I am, for God has blessed me with a brain that envisions things from beginning to end. He simply deposited a picture of the vision in my heart and brain. Amazing what my little brain can hold sometimes! Mind you, I saw confirmation time after time that this recovery process could work.

In 2007, the vision began to emerge out of the darkness into the light. The bloom was beginning to appear. This was a year of remarkable growth. It was gratifying to see what the NightShift team had accomplished since its humble beginnings in 2004. This was the first year we were really able to get focused and organized. Fruit blossomed when we weren't ducking spears and fighting distractions. We took advantage of this reprieve and got to work.

The ministry's team expanded in response to our growth and demand. God brought in predominately part-time volunteers to fill the roles of receptionist, general office and warehouse duties, and food and supplies coordinator. Thank You, Lord, for hearing our prayers for hands, feet, and especially hearts. Meanwhile, God provided me with buckets of grace and a fast-track education in working with volunteers.

The Surrey Leader published another article in September 2007. The tide was beginning to turn. This time Kevin Diakiw did not have to report on the harsh criticism of the city and the business and residential community towards our outreach services. His article was positive. Refreshing to see God's favour publicized after four years of blood, sweat, and tears.

Diakiw summed up 2007 and covered the challenges of the previous years:

It's been going on for the past four years. They're here to be fed, hear some caring words, and share in prayer. Whalley's downtrodden, many mentally ill, others battling drug addiction. But new faces are arriving: the young and the newly poor. The need for her service is growing, with nightly crowds four times the size of four years ago. Along with the growth in size, the ministry now has 437 volunteers and an 8,000-square-foot office in the 10700-block 135 Street Whalley. After a rough start because of community and city resistance, the idea gained momentum with several groups, including churches, residents, and businesses signing on to help. Connor's five-year plan now includes "Hope (Care) Cottages," a recovery facility for men and women; NightShift campus for long-term recovery; and private Christian homes with employment support and supervision. She knows that vision will have a hefty price tag, and is planning a fundraiser this month to help make the dream become reality.

We accomplished an amazing amount of work with our volunteer team. We organized the administrative functions that were absolutely necessary to develop structure, process, and order. The donor and volunteer database projects were completed, with the capability of monthly reporting and broadcast email communication. We got serious about special events, marketing, communications, and fundraising to raise the money required by the rapidly growing ministry. A new face for our website was developed. A Hope Builder campaign was launched in a local Christian newspaper, encouraging people to donate one dollar a day to the ministry.

NightShift's first annual corporate fundraising event, the Gala of Light, raised almost $40,000. Our third annual Saving Our Streets (SOS) event was held at Bible Fellowship Foursquare Church in November, where three hundred people were entertained by worship leader and author Andy Park and group, while participating churches and volunteers served curbside dishes —"meals on the street."

Meanwhile, at our NightShift offices, we were quickly discovering that we needed more than our cramped 2,000 square feet of space. We were in desperate need of warehouse storage and sorting space for the enormous amount of food and clothing donations that flowed steadily through the door. And thanks to a little serendipity, an additional 6,000 square feet became available next door. Once again, we were able to negotiate a sweet deal. But there was one major hurdle to jump through. We didn't have the money to do this massive renovation. So we did all that we could. We prayed for a miracle.

And guess what?

One of our local pastors invited me to lunch to meet two gentlemen visiting from a church in Florida. Over lunch, as was customary, I did what I love to do: share NightShift's story. When I came to the part about our proposed expansion, one of the men interrupted me.

"Excuse me, ma'am," he asked, "but how are you gonna get all that work done?"

With a smile, I came back with my standard answer, "I don't know, sir, but God does."

With that, he leaned over intently—I love it when they lean over like that—and replied, "Well, ma'am, I think we might just be able to help God with this chore."

I sat back in my chair, crossed my arms and legs, and smiled thoughtfully, singing "Alleluia!" under my breath.

The Florida church had an Extreme Mission Team, eighty youths accompanied by twenty-four adults, who travelled all over the world every summer, performing song, dance, and drama. While in town, they blessed each community by doing extreme projects. And in God's good timing, they just happened to be coming to our little town that year.

"Ma'am, we're here this week looking for a place to help. Could NightShift be our new project?" Hallelujah dancing! "We'll be in town in one month's time."

Stop the music! How were we going to swing that one? We had zero in the treasure chest. In spite of what I saw in the natural, I was sure God had a plan. It's fun saying that: God had a plan.

The deal went down like this. The Florida church supplies the labour, tools and a large percentage of the materials. We provide the finances for any other materials, if necessary, to complete the project. I went to work. Fast. One of our board members found a donor for material costs. We were set to go, but one week before the Extreme Team's arrival, I had to place the call to the church in Florida.

The money that had been promised to us by the board member had gone sideways. Excitement fizzled to despair. We asked God that if this was His will, He would make a way. If not, close the door. And it looked like the door had been closed.

I placed the call.

Twenty-four hours later, I got a call back.

"Ma'am," he said from Florida. "Our board met today. We're coming anyway. Don't worry about the money. It's all covered."

A massive bus rolled up to our doorstep, and eighty youths and twenty-four adults spilled out on the sidewalk carrying their bags of tools and supplies. An extreme team of one hundred people crawled over our space and worked tirelessly for four long days. Thereafter, volunteers, supplies, and donations poured through the doors to complete the project. A number of our street friends, who were skilled tradesmen, faithfully and tirelessly donated their time to help complete the taping, drywall, and painting. Bless their servant hearts and willingness to give back. When the dust had almost settled, God marshalled in a renovation contractor, who generously donated his heart, time, staff, materials, and expertise to professionally complete the job. Three rooms for prayer ministry and counselling services, four additional ministry offices and boardroom, space for storage and sorting for NightShift's outreaching distribution were completed by December.

How's that for a miracle?

DISCUSSION QUESTIONS

1. **Can you wait?**
   - Are there times when you are frustrated and want 'to wrap things up'?
   - What does the Bible say about waiting? Do you know how to wait? Are you willing to learn how to wait?
   - Describe a time when waiting and hoping has been what you needed.

2. **Do you fear giants?**
   - How do you see obstacles? As giants, or merely as challenges that can be overcome with God's help?
   - What are the giants in your life?
   - How have you overcome them?
   - Where does God fit in with the overcoming?

3. **Where are you discouraged in your life?**
   - What do you do when you are discouraged?

4. **Where are you courageous in your life?**

Chapter 19

MIRACLES

W E WERE STILL restricted by a City of Surrey bylaw that prohibited NightShift—a not-for-profit—from offering services to the community. You may recall that NightShift was not permitted to serve anyone from the street from inside our building because of this bylaw. We fastidiously adhered to this restriction and respected the city's decision. After all, we were no longer outlaws defending our right to feed the homeless; we were friends with the city, grateful for the spirit of cooperation shown by the new mayor, Dianne Watts.

We created Sisters Marketplace Inc. (eventually renamed Sisters Thrift Boutique) as a for-profit business, therefore exempt from the bylaw. Launched in late 2007, located in over 4,000 square feet in our building, Sisters sold higher-end donated clothing at rock-bottom prices. Sisters also had a trendy café that provided beverages as shoppers sashayed throughout the store.

Sisters became an important part of the ministry's strategy, enabling us to offer a place for the homeless to be counselled and receive prayer during the daytime. It soon became the day shift of our nightshift services. Part-time volunteers and one paid staff member ministered tirelessly to the needs of our homeless friends and people from the community. People with special needs and those in recovery or on parole who wanted to give back to the community volunteered in the store.

A pilot project, Sisters tested the feasibility of future social enterprise initiatives as potential revenue streams for NightShift's outreach programs. The generous space in the back of the Sisters store provided the perfect setting to present a worship evening, often featuring local worship bands. We called this service NightLife, a place where church and the street community gathered to worship God together. The place rocked with people singing and dancing, unaware that two cultures, homeless and not homeless, joined together oblivious to their observable differences. It was the way it's supposed to be. Here we are all the same. There were nights that the Holy Spirit's presence was so thick, I could barely stand. Oh, what a feeling! We were doing church.

Another piece of our Care Vision was the Isaiah 61 truck, a donated truck that would eventually offer mobile counselling and prayer ministry services. Renovations commenced in the summer of 2007. Two private companies donated a side door, windows, and translucent ceiling panels. A few years later the Isaiah 61 truck would be replaced with the Care Bus, a donated RV that was converted into a mobile unit offering street-level nursing, one-on-one prayer, a licensed counsellor, and referral and library services.

God continued to provide. Two businessmen braved the messiness of our renovations while I did my best to present our Care Vision plan amidst the chaos. God touched their hearts in a mighty way. They gave extravagantly. Without their generosity, our expansion dream and the rollout of the third phase of our Care Vision plan would not have materialized. One gentleman designated $50,000 specifically to cover the rent for Sisters Marketplace for one year.

That was a gigantic amount for this little ministry. I wonder if he realizes the impact. How far-reaching his gift and the ripple effect went in contributing to kingdom work. One night, while gathered around a table in Sisters café, two of our workers presented "Share Jesus Without Fear," an evangelical tool, to one of our street guys. I stood to the side, quietly praying, and watched a miracle unfold. This poor soul was in pain, struggling with addictions. Step by step, with the guidance of the Holy Spirit, the workers walked this man through the Bible. The scriptures spoke straight to his heart like a laser, about the truth of Jesus Christ, Son of God. I had the blessing and holy privilege to witness his "aha" moment. The lightbulb came on. Revelation! He accepted Jesus, weeping peacefully.

What's the ROI on that donor's $50,000 investment? What's one life worth? How do you place a value on the joy deposited in those two workers, the saints whom God used to bring this prodigal to the truth?

I can tell you this. My joy was indescribable. Eternal life. Priceless.

That year, 2007, the ministry received a total of $350,000 in financial donations. The value of gift-in-kind goods and volunteer labour doubled that amount. An astonishing amount of work was completed with those gifts. God multiplied them tenfold. You might recall that the donations received in 2004, our first year of operation, amounted to $13,000. "… All your needs according to the riches in glory in Christ Jesus" (Phil. 4:19 NIV).

The next year, 2008, brought joy, joy, joy, joy down in our hearts! God opened the doors to the extraordinary. It was as if the sun broke through a very dark cloud of oppression.

We basked in God's rays as we kept busy, settling into our new home and preparing for kingdom work.

Our focus was to get organized. I have never seen a team of people like this before—so motivated, so passionate, so ready to step up to the plate and serve Jesus. We had Joshua, Mary, David, and Martha hearts rolled all into one. Serving joyfully together, doing happy dances! We were bursting at the seams with people wanting to give of themselves to help the cause.

We got serious about completing the renovations to the Care Centre—the third phase of our vision plan offering prayer ministry and counselling. By September, believe it or not, I enrolled in full-time studies at Pacific Life Bible College for an intense, gruelling year of professional counsellor training. I know it sounds impossible but when God calls, I answer. He had placed that desire in my heart in 1986, the year I met Jesus, the first time the idea of becoming a counsellor was seeded in my heart.

This counselling training proved to be an invaluable tool in helping to develop the foundational structure of our Care Vision.

Meanwhile, we quietly served our homeless friends under the streetlights on 107th Avenue, well out of the public spotlight, for almost three years. Hallelujah! But we were dislodged once again. Smack in the middle of a cold, snowy winter.

It so happened that the adjacent property on 107th—I think it's a recreation centre now—was under construction to house the Volunteer Preparation Centre for the Olympics. The Olympic Committee and the city didn't think it was a good idea for the eyes of the world to see the homeless on the same street. It turned out that the Volunteer Preparation Centre was never used. It just sat empty.

Nevertheless, we were moved again around the corner to a parking lot on 135th Street, but that worked out just fine for us. We were given permission to serve literally right outside our front door. God is good.

Then, another believe-it-or-not, I joined the board of directors for the Downtown Surrey Business Association (DSBIA), formerly known as the Whalley Business Improvement Association, and served on its Safety Committee. The WBIA, can you imagine? God does have a sense of humour.

Meanwhile, the ministry was growing by leaps and bounds. Just when we were getting comfortable, we were squeezed again for more space. Our administration area was so packed that we took advantage of the loft area and built offices for Carmen and me away from the busyness.

With our heads and hearts together, we buckled down to administrative duties: preparing street policies and a procedural manual, code of conduct agreements, regular monthly leaders meetings, and newsletters. We never stopped. We also launched a monthly volunteer training program, Forge Equipping, to train workers in conflict resolution, communications, prayer ministry, addictions, and mental health. We waded into Personal Support Training and Team Building Training to help round out our team and work together seamlessly.

God continued providing us with the necessary funds to make ends meet. We developed a fundraising strategy and pursued our initiatives, such as the NightShift Golf Classic and the Gala of Light events. Just when our one-ton truck used for outreach services limped its final mile, God brought an almost-new truck our way, donated by a faithful volunteer.

Our Youth and Young Adult Outreach (YAYA) program took off. We termed it "AOK" for "acts of kindness." A team of students from Trinity Western University helped launch the program. Before long, more youths from local churches and schools joined them, carrying knapsacks packed with thermoses filled with hot chocolate, granola bars, care kits, and Bibles to people on the street. Our YAYAs, full of passion for the poor and homeless, are the future of the ministry.

For two years, it was miracle, after miracle, after miracle. Then the roof caved in. Literally.

DISCUSSION QUESTIONS

1. **Do you believe in miracles?**
   - What miracles are you a part of?
   - What miracles would want to be a part of?

Chapter 20

HOME AT LAST

MEANWHILE AS I juggled my counselling studies and ministry duties at NightShift, the dark clouds moved back in and the rains came. The roof caved. And we were under water. The floods came from overhead, from the ceiling everywhere, with a waterslide in the back of Sisters Marketplace. Why they call this an act of God, I don't know. It wasn't God but the enemy at play here.

Unfortunately, our landlords didn't share the same passion that we have for kingdom work. They looked the other way. Talk about conflict resolution. I had lots of opportunity to practice my "Come at it with the opposite spirit" lesson! But resolution was not forthcoming, nor were repairs. We were in serious trouble—up to our ankles—like Noah, but without an ark or a rainbow.

We had to move again!

Yep, you heard it right. After all the work, the blood, sweat, and tears—not to mention money—we were moving on again. This is beginning to sound like the new Willie Nelson NightShift road song, "On the road again. Just can't wait to get on the road again."

Our place had an extremely unhealthy ventilation system, no heat, no air conditioning, mould, and a roof that kept filling up what seemed like a swimming pool in the back of our Sisters store. Our landlords—can I say this, being an ordained minister and all?—were deadbeats. They just wouldn't carry out the repairs to correct the deficiencies as per our lease. Sorry. My mother taught me, "If you can't say anything nice about someone, don't say anything at all." Sound advice. So deadbeat is as nice as I can be!

We were stretched to the limit on finances. We went into January substantially 'in the red'. There was no way we could afford this move and underwrite the cost of renovating a new location. We'd barely settled into our current space. We were happy there. Do I hear discouragement? So we got praying! Big time. God, help us.

Once again, in faith, we stepped out on that proverbial limb. Well, *cliff* might be more descriptive. Sometimes I call Papa my cliff-hanging God. I'm sure that's not theologically sound but sometimes it sounds just right. This was one of those times.

But with God's help, we found the perfect place. Guess where? The same building that I stood looking at when we were evicted from the Mennonite parking lot. If you recall, I had asked God for the building in my prayer that night. Beamriders had left, gone out of business. Five years later, my prayer was answered. God is redemptive.

The new building meant that we had to downsize from 8,700 to 4,700 square feet. It was critical that we space-planned and were creative in our layout to maximize every square inch. Talk about flex-space! Renovations were extensive. We experienced roadblocks and unexpected costs due to permit requirements from the City of Surrey's Planning, Building, and Fire Departments. The original $100,000 projected budget swelled to $200,000. We didn't have any money in the bank account. It was an impossible fundraising task for the ministry to undertake in a challenged economy and in a very short period of time.

Good thing we had Someone to count on.

We called this move our Mission Possible, another one of NightShift's amazing "miracle stories." God provided every step of the way and brought an unexpected $100,000 in three different installments, just when we needed it. The witness of God's provision to those witnessing these renovations was tremendous. We "struck the ground" looking for donated labour and materials for the balance, and that was a full-time job in itself. Love and donations poured in!

I remember years before, that first Christmas at Pastor Steen's old Foursquare Church where it all started, standing outside the shelter one night during the wee hours of the morning, I stressed over why we didn't have more hands or money to help the cause. Across the street, a new townhome development was under construction, and some units were already occupied. The new development's presence was a nightly reminder of the life I used to live, especially the homebuilding industry from which I was exiting. I was struck with the stark contrast.

Homebuilders were building new homes for those who had the means to achieve the comforts of home, while others were perishing in extreme poverty just across the street. Steps away from these new homes, people were sleeping on a cold concrete floor with no place to call home. Next to the development, the Scotia Bank Tower loomed in the darkness, its brightly lit offices boasting corporate prosperity. As I gazed up at all the lit windows, I was struck with the dichotomy between rags and riches—the display of materialism beside the cesspool of misery where I stood.

I thought then as I do now: at what point does society assume responsibility?

I believe it starts with us, with you and me. Even when we hurt. Even when the odds are against us. Are you ready?

How about corporate Canada? Where is your corporate social responsibility? I understand the concept of business as a profit-maker, making money, and donating some proceeds to charity. That had long been my mantra, but now I realize it takes more than money to turn the tide on poverty. Government funding has done little to alleviate social problems; if anything, it has created a "helping industry" that perpetuates the problem. By making no one accountable—neither agency nor client—the problems will never change.

I envisioned something different, perhaps something a little idealistic, but why not? What would it look like if businesses took the lead? What if corporations worked together with social agencies and the faith community to provide holistic solutions to dispel the problem of poverty and addictions? What if business principles were integrated with faith and the best clinical practices to transform the plight of the poor? What if homebuilders and developers who were providing homes for those who could afford a home, gave back to those who didn't have a roof over their heads?

At NightShift, we've had a taste of this—just a toe in the ocean—but I can tell you the concept works. It works for the homeless and it's starting to make a change in the lives of our street friends.

We've seen the ministry grow over the last seven years with a continuous revenue increase from $13,000 in 2004 to $800,000 in 2011, nearly all of it through private and corporate donations, including the homebuilding industry! This is a huge testimony of God's amazing blessing and favour! We are now focusing on our continued self-sustainability by developing a Ministry Development Department that strategically searches out funding opportunities to help with our increased capital and operational costs. I am often asked to speak about our ministry's Care Vision to corporate groups and churches.

Allow me to bless you with a story about how God placed $100,000 in my hands for our renovations. The story is true, though it sounds a little like a Hollywood movie.

I was having a not-so-good day on a weekend. Tired and discouraged, I decided to treat myself with a manicure. It's a girl thing! I didn't have the budget I'd had in my past life but, hey, sometimes a girl has to do what a girl has to do.

I'm sitting in the massage chair, staring into space, feeling sorry for myself. The next thing I know, the girl next to me starts up a conversation. A God-ordained conversation. We hit it off right away. We had tons in common. Both loved the Lord. Both in full-time ministry. God placed a bubble around us as we chatted and—to make a long story short—we ended up praying, right there in the nail salon, in front of all to see, oblivious to what was happening around us. We became friends. Fast.

Within the month, she and her friend attended an information session and joined me afterwards in our prayer circle outside with our street friends. During the prayer, my head bowed, my eyes closed, I felt someone silently coming alongside me. It was my friend. She smiled at me as she placed something in my jacket pocket, saying, "Don't lose that." And she returned to prayer in the circle. Later, I found their $20,000 cheque. Things like that never happen to me! I was speechless! God knew our need and supplied it, right on time. And look how He did it. In a nail salon! Wow. He just loves to surprise His kids with out-there gifts.

It gets better. Between Christmas and New Year's, I was having dinner with my new friends in a busy restaurant. I was chatting away as usual about the ministry, discussing our plans for the renovations.

They ask, "What's your renovation budget?"

To which I replied, "$100,000."

In the end, our costs ended being doubled, which is pretty typical for renovation budgets. Her friend leans forward, looks me straight in the eye, and says, "We'd like to give you half of it."

I wasn't sure I had heard him correctly. It was really loud in that restaurant. So I answered, "Half of what?" Don't laugh, that's what I said!

His eyes shone, "Half of your renovation costs."

I still didn't get it. Okay. Things like this don't happen to me every day. I was shell-shocked, stunned, stupid-silly. Those who know me rarely see me without words. But this was one of those times. All I could do was stare at him. Blankly. He leaned over again and said plainly, so I would get it clearly this time, "$50,000."

I didn't know whether to laugh, cry, or pass out. I chose to cry. I burst into tears. Shamelessly in the middle of the restaurant. No decorum. I didn't care. The God of the universe had just given me another big fat kiss on the check. Actually, both cheeks! God's little ministry desperately needed the funds. And He made the deposit. Again. This was an answer to prayer! We did the hallelujah dance at the ministry for days. Remember, I met this friend in a nail salon! God has a sense of humour.

Wait, it gets better. I'm in a restaurant with my girlfriend again having dinner. She had just returned from a trip away and had brought a gift for me. A beautiful handbag. Admiring it, I dug in the bag, pulled out a piece of paper, thought it was the receipt, and tossed it on the table, being polite not to look at it. She didn't say a word. She just sat there, calmly smiling at me. She's like that a lot. We were talking with another girl I hadn't seen in years. This other girl picked up the slip of paper from the table, looked at it, put it down, looked intently at me, and said, "Umm, you might want to look at that paper."

Curious, I picked it up. It wasn't a receipt. Silly! It was a cheque for $30,000. What! Am I glad I didn't crumble up that receipt! What an awesome God we serve! I'm still dancing about that one. And to think I get to tell the stories! We needed exactly $30,000 to meet the costs to complete our renovations. Of course! "And my God will meet all your needs according to the riches of his glory in Christ Jesus" (Phil. 4:19 NIV). The Bible says *all* of our needs, not some.

I'm grinning like a Cheshire cat telling you this story. Don't we have fun serving the Most High God?

God provided all the money to meet our renovation expenses: cash and gift-in-kind donations as well as funds gathered at our special events. But the lack of finances to employ and keep qualified staff with solid administrative and ministry experience was a constant challenge. We had a major staff turnover that summer, with three part-time staff stepping away within weeks of one another. They left for larger ministries offering full-time salaries and benefits, leaving major gaps in some critical areas in our ministry that needed immediate action.

Following the departure of the three staff members and just before our renovations in our new space kicked off, Carmen, my dear sister in the Lord, my executive assistant and right-hand person, was diagnosed with stage-three breast cancer. She immediately vacated her position to start intensive medical treatment.

I was heartbroken for her personally, and her departure left me spinning professionally. I was in a crisis state, with basically no one to help. No one to step into her shoes, no one with her experience and knowledge of the ministry. Carmen handled responsibility equivalent to three persons. As I said previously, she was a trooper—going over and beyond to do whatever it took to keep things going. (Towards the end of her treatment, she thankfully stepped back into the ministry slowly, with a plan to ease back into full-time duties. I don't have the words to express how grateful we are to God for bringing her through this trying time. Healed! Another big miracle.)

But her departure forced us to readjust quickly. We were sucker-punched. I was not going to take this blow sitting down. So I got up, pulled my boots on, tightened my belt, adjusted my armour, slapped on my helmet, lifted my sword and shield, and lunged back with the Word. God was watching my back. He brought a lifesaver. A part-time consultant stepped in—the Business-Sitter. Like the trooper she is, she joined with me to combat this emergency crisis management. We rolled up our sleeves, got to work, and began the process of restructuring the ministry on a shoestring budget, without the hiring of additional full-time employees. *Whew.* It felt like we were climbing an insurmountable mountain. Position scopes and job responsibilities were redefined and adjusted, a workable organizational chart as well as a branding and marketing plan for NightShift developed, the Care Centre and Sisters Thrift Boutique (formerly Marketplace) were fine-tuned, and an online collaborative management system was established. Technology and social media came to NightShift: cost-effective electronic newsletters, blogs, Twitter, an updated Sisters Thrift Boutique website, and a new initiative, Sisters Thrift Boutique online store, all of which have proved to be very successful. The Business-Sitter was a godsend.

And to think we moved into a new location with all that stress and chaos! We made it through with the help of a team of recovery guys and faithful volunteers. God provided a truck and all the hands and feet needed. Even pizza. For months we climbed over boxes, sidestepped files, tramped on bags, dug through carton after carton looking for phones, computers, staplers, you name it. We didn't have time to unpack. There was kingdom work to do. It was a season of organized disorganization.

We limped through the year, and I mean limped, with a skeleton team of volunteers and a few paid part-time staff, juggling duties as they flew at us. The bank balance was in an all-time low. I was getting very adept in creative financing. Or, as I was often heard saying, "Robbing Peter to pay Paul." Which I know is not scriptural or a good accounting practice, for that matter. But it got us through! We kept our hands on the plough and never looked back. There's a saying, "When things get tough, the tough get going." That totally epitomized our faithful team. It was over-the-top stressful but we pressed on. This wasn't a job to this team. This was service! We were acutely aware that we were serving our King. Our reward was in heaven! "Don't be fooled by what they say" (2 Thess. 2:3 NLT). I encouraged the team continually with a slightly different version, "Do not be discouraged by what we see." God has everything under control. God honours faithfulness and tenacity.

We gathered a team of ministry and industry professionals who served on an advisory committee that met regularly for almost a year to establish a firm foundation for our licensed Christian counselling centre. This dedicated team worked on ethics, branding, forms, process, and everything you could think of, to make sure our i's were dotted and our t's crossed to create a ministry within a ministry.

We brought on a full-time Care Centre director, her salary subsidized by a grant, a woman ideal for the job. She is a Mary heart through and through. We were awarded another small grant, which helped us to further our planning and research for the Care Centre and Care Bus projects.

We became very intentional in looking at ways to increase our revenue stream. The ministry's demands were growing daily but our funds lagged behind the need. We've learned from experience that this is the main way the enemy tries to take us out. Attack our finances. Relentlessly. With purpose, we identified potential funders and got busy writing grant proposals. In the future, our goal is to engage a full-time person who can dedicate full-time effort to source available funds.

I have two sayings I repeat to the team on a pretty regular basis. "If you don't ask, you don't get." " You have not because you ask not" (James 4:2 NIV). And "Look at the birds of the air; they do not sow or reap or store away in barns, and yet your heavenly Father feeds them" (Matt. 6:26 NIV).

Here's my humble interpretation. He feeds the birds, but He doesn't bring the food and drop it in their mouths.

He provides for it, but they have to go find it. That's my theology. Not sure if you agree, but I think we have to do our part. And that we're doing, enthusiastically and with accountability, being good stewards of what God has provided the ministry.

We were awarded a corporate grant that enabled us to engage a leadership development director. This position focuses on mobilizing our forever-increasing and essential NightShift volunteer force. The coordinator recruits internally and externally, screens, evaluates, trains, encourages, equips, and releases people into ministry positions. Our goal is to establish an "internship" program eventually, to capture and encourage young adults to serve alongside key ministry volunteers and staff with an eye to the future planting of NightShift into other communities and cities across Canada. And who knows? Perhaps one day, beyond.

God had a plan, and after we wiped the sweat off our brows and breathed, we realized that this location was a blessing. We had stepped into a new era for NightShift. We could all feel it. The new location turned out to be a very strategic move for the ministry, the counselling centre, and the store. It had curb appeal and good community presence. We settled in once again and made it our home. "You intended to harm me, but God intended it for good to accomplish what is now being done, the saving of many lives" (Gen. 50:20 NLT).

Our purse strings were beyond stretched that summer. There were no funds in the bank to pay staff or rent. It was hard to keep my eyes on Jesus. I couldn't see a way out. My assistant at the time was noticeably stressed, "We're going to miss payroll!" It sure looked probable "in the natural." I felt God's nudge. Sighing, I put my poker face on and spoke with as much confidence as I could muster, "Prepare the cheques. I'll sign them. Give them to every staff member. They continually give their all to this ministry and they don't need to worry about their paycheques. God will come through!"

In truth, I felt nauseous. She backed out of my office with an incredulous look and did as she was instructed to do. I sent an arrow prayer, "Help God! Please help!"

The following afternoon, one of my board members brought in a businessman to introduce him to the ministry and tour our new facilities. We were cultivating and encouraging potential partners to support the Care Vision. Once again, I shared the Lord's vision, using my humble vision board. When I came to the part of the Care Cottages and Village, I could see God touching his heart. He leaned over. You just know I was smiling when he did that.

He said, "When you get to the part of the cottages and village. Let me know. That's when I want to be involved."

I leaned back in my chair, folded my arms and crossed my legs, and smiled. You've seen me to do this a few times before.

Then he continued, "Until then, I'd like to give you a small donation today."

Leaning forward in my chair, I gratefully said, "Thank you!" Honestly, I was expecting $100, somewhere in that vicinity.

He continued, "It's not much. $10,000. Is that okay?"

I literally dropped my head on the table. Remember my God-bumps? I burst into tears. He had no way of knowing that $10,000 was the precise amount we needed for the payroll cheques I had signed the day before. Another kiss on the cheek from Papa. And He added a few winks! I could sense angels doing high-fives all around me! He honours faith. And obedience. He promised to provide. And He did.

Faith-builder!

DISCUSSION QUESTIONS

1. **Describe a time in your life when you have been met with despair and believed all was lost only to find hope or an answer to your prayers?**

2. **When does society assume responsibility for people who are disadvantaged?**
   - How do you and your community accept responsibility for 'the least of these'?
   - What do you feel about the integration of business and works of faith?
   - What role can businesses play? Can business and faith coexist? If so, why?
   - What business do you know that has taken the lead to give back to the community in which they work?

3. **What are you asking God for in your life?**
   - Are there any rewards for serving 'the least of these'?
   - What have been yours?

4. **Do you believe God honours faith and obedience?**
   - Are you willing to be faithful and obedient to God?
   - What do faith and obedience mean to you?
   - How do you bring this to your own service/ministry/volunteering/life?

Chapter 21

VISION BECOMES REALITY

———————————————————◆

I THOUGHT I'D blown it. Early in 2011, we held a pastors and church leaders appreciation luncheon. Our training area in our new building was transformed—white table-cloths, candles, and flowers. A very different atmosphere from what we do in that space for our evening street service. This get-together was an introduction to our new Centre and marked the unofficial grand opening of the Care Centre and Care Bus.

Using my original vision board—it's been brought out for a lot of presentations since 2007—I presented the Care Vision to the gathering. You might remember that the vision board is a visually designed graphic that takes the viewer through the six steps of our Care Vision, from the first contact on the street to the long-term recovery centre for addictions known as the Care Village.

With the aid of the vision board, guests could see and understand the six-phased plan that God had dropped into my heart years previously. It is a big plan and when presenting, I watch the faces of the attendees carefully to judge their level of acceptance. For most, this is a dream way too big to come true. But God told me to dream big, and I do.

The meeting with the pastors and church leaders at the candlelit luncheon was going well but when I reached the Care Village phase, I became unsure and discomposed. Maybe I was a little frightened that my colleagues would also think my dreams were too large.

I said I wasn't sure when the Care Village would materialize, but I had a sense it wouldn't be too far off in the future. Then I tried a little joke.

Humour, as you probably know, can be dangerous. When you can make people laugh, you're more likely to sway them. But when a joke falls flat, your purpose is just as likely to fall with it.

This being a pastorate gathering, I made a biblical reference to Psalm 50:10, in which God proclaims that, "... for every animal of the forest is mine, [as are] the cattle on a thousand hills."

"If He wants the village to happen," I said, "all it would take is for Him to kill a couple cows!"

There was dead silence. I mean, dead. It came out of my mouth before I realized what I was saying. I wondered then how many more months or years I'd set back the vision that God had given me.

Following the meeting, Pastor Steve Witmer approached me, a thoughtful expression on his face. He asked, "Mac, does the village have to be situated on a property located nearby?"

"Why, no," I answered quickly. "No, as a matter of fact it would be preferable if it was out of Dodge. We want to take people away from their source of pain for a season. The further away the better."

"I have an idea," he said. "Can we discuss it tomorrow, that's if you're not too busy rustling our Father's cattle?"

The next day as I entered his office, Pastor Witmer stood up from his desk, removed a picture from his wall, and handed it to me. The first thing I saw was a landing strip for a plane, then a grouping of houses, big and small. I was puzzled.

"What's this?" I asked.

With a smile, he answered my question with one of his own.

"Do you think this could work for the Care Village?" he asked. "It's five hundred and eighty acres in Fort St. John. Far enough out of Dodge?"

Lost for words, blubbering like a baby, tears streaming down my face, I couldn't answer.

"Do you want me to answer for you?" Pastor Steve teased. With one word, he brought God's vision into reality. He said, "Yes!"

Then he painted the picture.

"It's located in a beautiful, natural setting on pristine meadowland, surrounded on two sides by the sparkling waters of the beautiful Graham River, a view of the Rocky Mountains and the foothills in the distance," he said. "It's approximately one hour's flight from Vancouver, followed by a two-hour drive on a well-maintained road, the last six kilometres on a gravel provincial road. It's situated northwest of Fort St. John, in an area well known for its gas and oil exploration. The property is accessible by air with a mile-long landing strip accommodating small-to-medium aircraft.

"Currently, on the site there are three two-storey homes, two single-storey homes, a large dining hall and classroom building, a woodworking/mechanical shop, and a variety of smaller outbuildings."

I remained speechless.

"The property was established originally as a Christian community in 1972 and reached a maximum occupancy of 160 people," he explained. "Each family had its own home but shared most meals, work duties, church, and for the children, a Christian school. A church movement formed the organization with roots in Amish, Mennonite, United Brethren, and other Christian backgrounds. The early emphasis was to create a godly culture for the families and to be as agriculturally self-sufficient as possible."

I couldn't say anything.

"At present, the property is held in the name of South Fork Christian Society, with the stated purpose of advancing God's kingdom, which is pretty much the same business you're in."

I raced back to the office with the picture of the property in my hand. I flew through the front door and plunked the photo down on the front desk. Happy dancing!

The team celebrated, but I suddenly became quiet and in a whispered conversation with God, reality struck. "This is great, Father," I said, "but we don't have any money to do this village now."

Oh, ye of little faith.

The words weren't out of my mouth when the phone rang. "Someone looking to speak to you," I was informed by our receptionist.

I all but skipped down the hall, uncertain about the money but excited about the possibility. In my office, I discovered that the caller was a former client who had given us our very first donation of one thousand dollars seven years before. I hadn't heard from him for the last six years but he'd been on my heart for months. I'd placed a yellow sticky note with his name on it on my office wall as a reminder to call him.

I said excitedly, "Hey, I can't believe we're speaking. I was just thinking about you two days ago."

"Well, I too was just thinking of you two days ago," he replied.

Coincidence? Just being nice?

"Look," he continued, "if you receive a cheque for two hundred and fifty thousand dollars at the end of the month, please know it's from me."

Clearing my throat, I tried to sound calm. "Pardon? Two hundred and fifty thousand dollars? A quarter-million-dollar cheque?"

"Yep," he answered.

I felt the smile in his voice over the telephone lines.

After two trips to the property in Fort St. John with two board members and a team from the ministry, and tons of prayer seeking God for direction, we made the decision to cautiously proceed with initial renovations of the Men's House. God apparently heard our prayers, for not long after, Pastor Steve approached me with something else to consider.

Adjacent to Bible Fellowship Church is a three-acre property, which might be made available to NightShift for the Care Cottage Community, if we wanted to go through a feasibility process to determine its suitability. Not only did we have one prayer answered, but God also brought another opportunity for us to consider at the same time. And just to sweeten the pot further, while we examined our options on the Care Cottage property, God fetched a businessman—incidentally the same man who had given us the $10,000 donation the year before—who generously provided a beautiful, spacious log home on a four-acre property for us to use as a care home to test our vision.

The Surrey Leader headline on January 12, 2012, proclaimed: "Surrey-based NightShift Street Ministries is getting into the work of treating the addicted—A 'shift' in dealing with poverty. God told her to dream big."

Kevin Diakiw wrote in the *Leader*, "Beginning this weekend, four people will be moving into a test house for recovery in South Surrey on a four-acre parcel of land. The treatment is simple, using the same method Connor has employed since she started working with the homeless in 2004: Love people until they learn to love themselves."

I add to his story, "and until they love God!"

The project is a long way from Connor's humble beginnings in 2004 when her goal was simply to feed the homeless and share the Christian word of God with them. Back then, she operated out of the front of a church and when that came to the attention of the city, NightShift was ushered out. Now, NightShift has a 4,000-sq.-ft. office space on King George Boulevard that accommodates a boardroom, kitchen, counsellor offices, and Sisters Thrift Boutique (which now has it own IPhone app in which clothing can be reserved for purchase).

Beyond the local Care Cottage Community, she has a Care Village in the works in Fort St. John. Not long ago, she was telling someone about the Fort St. John property and he asked, "How are you going to get people there?" She thought bus was the most suitable and affordable way. "Nonsense," he said, "I've got a six-seater plane for you." Connor says she couldn't have dreamed of having things fall into place as they are.

God told me to dream big!

And she thanks God she didn't let her analytical thinking get in the way. "If I had thought this through, I wouldn't have done it," she says. "Do I regret it? Not for a second."

So here's the big picture for the local Care Cottages and Care Village: everyone benefits—the residents and volunteers, the local community, the donors and supporters. There is no segregation among those coming for healing regardless of income or status. People are treated with love, respect, and dignity. Residents and guests learn to cohabit regardless of their life circumstances and challenges.

The goal of the Care Village in Fort St. John is to integrate people from all walks of life to live together in harmony and acceptance and to love, serve, and support one another throughout the process. People experience an active lifestyle working the land and enjoying nature while contributing to the overall sustainability of the program. Healthy, nutritious food, grown organically, will help people regain their health and vitality. It is a place that offers counselling, education, recreation, training, and life and work skills.

The location had already housed a successful Christian-based community, and many of the buildings are still in good standing. There used to be a Youth With A Mission (YWAM) base on the land to which the students were flown from around the world to study discipleship training. The YWAM success rate is measured by how many students go into missions full-time after completing the program. There was an astonishing 80 percent success rate with students who trained in this community. The curriculum is the same around the world, so YWAM tried to figure out what was different about this base. They found that there was something special about the land and the location, in part because there were no distractions.

The Care Village offers a place of solitude for people to come together and connect with God, themselves, and other people—while they work through their life issues. It is a place where volunteers, teachers, professionals, residents, and families can live together—for up to two years—to serve and support one another in our life journeys. It is a place to enjoy nature and be still. "Be still and know that I am God" (Psalm 46:10 NIV).

In his book, *Discipleship Counselling*, Dr. Neil Anderson states, "There is no greater privilege than to be used by God to help others." He quotes an anonymous person who says,

"It is one of life's greatest compensations that no person can sincerely help another without helping him or herself in the process."

Our belief is that even the smallest effort, when multiplied by many people, has an enormous impact in making a difference in helping to guide people to a new, happy life.

Is the dream too big? Not for God, it isn't.

DISCUSSION QUESTIONS

1. **Are you willing to be used by God?**
   - How do you think God might want to use you?

2. **How can you love people until they learn to love themselves?**

Chapter 22

COINCIDENCE?

A DREAM FULFILLED, I graduated from Pacific Bible College with a Registered Professional Counsellor Diploma—at the same time the ceiling fell in, the floods came and the NightShift exodus was undertaken. The demands on my time and attention made 2009 and 2010 a blur and perhaps the most challenging years ever. Then again, haven't I said that about every year?

Difficult as it was, however, I rejoice: Bible college was a sacred, inspiring experience. I had travelled a long road to find this gift from God, a road that had begun with an extraordinary event three decades before—in a Nova Scotia hospital, New Year's, 1980.

I was in a semi-private room, my privacy maintained by a curtain that separated me from the patient lying in the other bed. Through the curtain, we talked, swapping our woeful tales about why we had landed in the hospital over the Christmas holidays. She was suffering from a tubal pregnancy; I with complications following a Caesarean-section delivery of my youngest daughter two weeks previously.

Then chaos struck. It happened so quickly. What seemed like seconds following our brief introduction, I could hear my neighbour frantically pushing the call button for a nurse. She was in a panic. But the panic was not for her. It was for me.

I was entirely unaware that my body was undergoing a massive postpartum hemorrhage. My uterus ruptured and I was bleeding out of control. As I fought unconsciousness, blood pooled and spilled over the starched sheets onto the spotless hospital floor. The hospital paging system screamed out an emergency code for a medical team.

Within minutes, my room was mayhem. In what seemed an eternity, a medical team hovered over me while more than fifteen units of blood pumped into my body, stabilizing me while we waited for a surgeon to arrive from a New Year's party. When he entered, he was clothed in his black tux. He hurriedly readied himself for surgery.

As I bled, my pulse dropped dangerously. I could feel myself leaving my body—to the right, upwards, toward the unknown. Each time I felt myself being pulled up and out, I called out to Brenda, the emergency nurse.

"I'm going somewhere …"

The pump that administered the IV blood transfusions into my body was not thumping quickly enough to stabilize blood levels. To assist the machine, a doctor, standing to my right, began pumping the blood into my veins with his bare hands. This happened repeatedly—doctor pumping, pulse restored, me leaving, more pumping, pulse restored, me leaving—until they finally rolled me out and down the corridor to the operating room.

An out-of-body experience, not frightening, but absolutely real. No, I was not afraid. In fact, it was peaceful. Surreal, I suppose. But I fought the pull: I had a new baby and a family at home who needed me.

Packed in ice to slow down the bleeding and after five hours in surgery, I emerged alive. Barely. I was not expected to live. A miracle had occurred. Acute massive transfusions and an emergency hysterectomy saved my life.

At the time, I was young, with no more than a Sunday school concept of God. The idea of the Holy Spirit entering my life was no more real to me than becoming an astronaut. I was a young mom with three kids and a normal life to live.

What I had no understanding of was the extraordinary coincidence that would irreversibly *shift* my life. Reflecting back now on that moment of life and death, I see that God wasn't finished with me.

There was a call on my life.

Of course, I am hardly the only person to have such a call. God has a plan and a purpose for all of our lives, sometimes in spite of ourselves. As Aimee Semple McPherson, evangelist and founder of the Foursquare Church, said, "If you have a pulse, God has a purpose for your life."

But my life was not normal when I returned from hospital. I look back on those years in Dartmouth, Nova Scotia, and see it now more calmly—as if all this had happened to someone else—but I also remember that at the time I was gripped by my pain and fear.

My second marriage had collapsed after six turbulent years drained by infidelity, drugs, and alcohol. Now it sounds a little like a bad country and western song, but I was much younger then, with little perspective and no spiritual understanding to sustain me. I was left a single mother with three children to support. It was up to me to carve out a life again on my own. As you know, I've confessed the fear that had gripped me most of my life—my fear of abandonment, of being alone. These days one might find help through a postpartum hemorrhage trauma support group, but back then in Dartmouth, Nova Scotia, I struggled with my demons alone—in a state of shock, paralyzed, frightened of life.

My 1986 journal records my terror:

I thought I was coping well with this separation. But the reality hits home. Tonight I can't sleep for fear. My stomach is gripped with a knot that just won't go away. Nothing I do can dissolve the sense of panic that controls me. I'm fearful this pain is just the beginning of another downward spiral. I want to crush it before it crushes me. I'm fearful that my recent letter to my husband—my attempt at being transparent and vulnerable—may have been too much for him. I'm fearful that it may result in his heart becoming hard if he really knew who I was behind my wall. I'm fearful that perhaps we can't communicate at a distance by letters. Then what? We can't even speak face-to-face without arguing. I'm fearful that he may decide that he doesn't love me anymore. He might discover that he can be content without me. That life is not that difficult without his family.

I was scared. So scared. Scared that this separation would be permanent ... that I was powerless to change the situation ... that sleep no longer came.

Tears are beginning to flow, without warning.

I remember how frightened I was that the tears would not stop ... of the headaches that struck like hammers on church bells when I wept ... that my face would reveal my anguish in the morning. I didn't want my children to see me like that.

But my deepest, secret fear was of losing control ... of slipping into a dark pit of depression. I was scared for my children, how this affected them. Scared for them if I became unglued and emotionally unstable. Scared that I didn't have answers to these questions.

What if I find it's unbearable to continue with the pressures of work and raising my children alone? Then what? Who will look after us? What if my husband meets someone else? How would I cope? My heart would be crushed beyond repair.

It aches now. Every week that passes, I feel more and more fearful that he'll replace me with another—someone who won't mind his excessive drinking or insist on him changing.

But then, it was also true that I was scared we might reconcile with nothing changed ... that I would cave—compromise—walk through a life with no respect, more emotional abuse, still more rejection, and pain.

The future, the fighting, the failure of my marriage, addiction to painkillers, that everyone will know, that people will nod with that look on their faces when they see a single mother with three children and pass judgment, that I would overlook the chaos of my marriage in order for us to stay together—I was afraid of it all. I wanted with all my heart to fix my life.

My husband had bolted to British Columbia. Several months after his departure, he reconnected, pressuring me to travel across the country to visit him for ten days. To be truthful, I was emotionally drained. Done—*fini!* I was convinced that nothing would repair the damage that had taken place in our marriage, but I felt duty-bound to visit, if at the very least to bring closure to the pain as well as the relationship.

We stayed with friends of my husband, a Christian family and their three children. The wife, a devout Christian and loving woman, welcomed me into her picture-perfect "Little House on the Prairie" home with warmth and love. This kind of love was a polar experience—like stepping onto another planet. My thirsty heart yearned for this life. I was encircled by laughter, love, kindness, respect, and joy. And God.

"Now I lay me down to sleep" was my childhood prayer each night. I loved God with a pure, childlike faith. I had met Him in Sunday school in a conservative United Church in Nova Scotia. I heard about His Son Jesus Christ and the Holy Spirit. But I didn't know Him intimately—not like my hostess did. I had never been around someone who radiated quiet peace and faith like this woman did. There was something different about her that drew me to her and her church.

During that short visit, I attended a Sunday morning church service at Bible Fellowship in Surrey. This church was like nothing I had ever experienced. The place was packed with people singing, clapping, and raising their hands—some speaking a strange language. Truthfully? I thought they were all crazy. My heart pounded. I wanted to run and hide. I definitely did not fit in here. Even my hair, my clothes were different.

Here is what I believed: these people were obviously good. Me? I was undeniably bad. My sinful life was fully exposed in stark contrast to these decent people. I was a mistake—a failure and a rejected woman, unloved, trudging through life negotiating yet another painful hurdle. I feared that I was exposed. *I must have stuck out like a sore thumb*, I thought, for after the service, chirpy people kept pouncing on me—worse, hugging me—welcoming me to the family. What family? Was this a cult?

Yet my heart was stirred by this love. Curious, I attended the evening service with my new friend, who was serving in the nursery. I bravely located a seat in the back of the church, making sure I sat alone. And waited. Under a bowed head, my doubting eyes darted back and forth, surveying every virtuous person around me. Five pastors in matching black suits, white shirts, and ties paraded single-file along the elevated platform in front of the musicians, sinking side by side onto chairs, just like Jimmy Swaggart, a Pentecostal American televangelist, and his cohorts. All the while, music played softly in the background. As they sat, their eyes travelled to and fro over the congregation.

I ducked my head.

The musicians and singers unexpectedly broke forth in jubilant ovation. People rose, shouting, dancing, and praising God. The place rocked in something they called *worship*! I stood with them, watching incredulously, hopeful that my shocked demeanour wasn't too obvious. I didn't join in with their singing for fear I'd get caught up in this strange force that would whisk me away to Neverland. I hung on to normalcy and fought against the tugging of the Spirit. Where was my quiet United Church minister, Sunday school teacher, pews, hymnbook, organ music, and choir?

After what felt like infinity, the music eventually settled into a slow, soft rhythmic beat. Love songs, they called them. I stood with my head bowed, wanting to run but unable to make my feet move …

I love You, Lord,
and I lift my voice
to worship You,
Oh, my soul, rejoice!
Take joy, my King,
in what You hear,
may it be a sweet,
sweet sound
in Your ear.

As much as I fought the urge to sing these words, something deep inside me started to break. What I didn't know then was that—six years before when I was near death, hemorrhaging in that Nova Scotia hospital—my husband had called out west to friends at this same church to pray for me. This same congregation had called upon God to save my life. Six years later, 6,100 kilometres from my life in Nova Scotia, I had been called to this same church in Surrey where I came face to face with Almighty God.

I started to whisper the lyrics of the love song.

"I love You, Lord, and I lift my voice, to worship you."

As I breathed the words, my voice became stronger. I began to sing.

"My life is a mess," my heart spoke to God as I sang, "… Oh, my soul rejoice …"

"They say You can do a better job," my heart spoke. "I can't do it anymore, not on my own. You can have it."

"… Take joy, my King, in what you hear …"

And as I sang out in joy, my spirit rose, and in that moment, I gave my heart to the Lord.

A few simple words of complete and desperate surrender. That's all it took. I didn't know the sinner's prayer. But my heart did. Something happened. The *shift*. I felt an intense heat travel from the top of my head down through to the tips of my toes. So mighty was this force that I couldn't remain standing. Powerless, I dropped to my seat. Confused, I thought I was going to pass out on the spot. What was this? God? At least He hadn't whisked me away to Neverland.

No one seemed to notice this overpowering event. No one. Except God and me.

I've spoken about this moment with others. Some believe I received conversion and the Holy Spirit baptism in one glorious sweep. Whatever it was, it was life altering. God did something totally unexpected and profound to catch my attention. I was a stubborn doubter. It worked. He absolutely got my attention. This *shift* was a major turnaround in my life. I haven't been the same since!

Six months later, my marriage reconciled. I packed up all my possessions and family and moved from my beloved Nova Scotia across the country to Surrey. I stepped into a new life with my husband, children, and God, eager to serve Him for the rest of my life and determined to make the marriage work. I wish I could say we lived happily ever after, but despite my best whole-hearted efforts, the marriage struggled for another five challenging years and eventually came to its inevitable and agonizing end.

Today Bible Fellowship is my home church. I'm an ordained Foursquare minister, a licensed professional counsellor, and a leader of God's ministry, NightShift Street Ministries. If that isn't a miracle, I don't know what is.

As I write this, my spirit soars. Something miraculous is taking place. The maintenance man in my townhome complex captures my attention as he quietly works outside my home-office window. He is melodically whistling my favourite and beloved love song.

I love You, Lord,
and I lift my voice
to worship You,
Oh, my soul, rejoice!

What are the chances? A kiss on the cheek from my Papa!

DISCUSSION QUESTIONS

1. **Do you believe God has a plan for you?**
   - At what point in time did you feel this?
   - To what did He call you?
   - What do you see as the first step to fulfilling God's plan and purpose for your life?
   - How have you run and hid from your life? From God?

2. **What is the plan that God has for your life?**
   - If there is no plan, why not?
   - What is God doing in your life 'in spite' of you?

3. **What does it mean to be obedient to God's calling?**

4. **Describe a time when you have felt powerless to change a situation.**
   - What was your deepest fear during that time of your life?

5. **Do you have a 'coincidence' story?**

Chapter 23

SWORD

O N A FOUR-HOUR flight to Vancouver recently, I sat next to a delightful young woman with her husband and adorable one-year-old son. As we chatted, she asked me the inevitable question, "What do you do?" I love answering that question! Then she asked why I did such a thing, especially after I had shared with her some of our inspiring but challenging story.

"I was just willing and obedient to God's calling," I explained.

The woman thought about that for a few minutes and turned to me and said, "I think it's more than that. You are more than just willing and obedient. You are courageous."

I don't consider myself that way, especially since I spent most of life running from fear. "Take courage and walk in My strength, not your own. Face every situation—head on—armed with the sword of the Spirit. You never need to turn back and run. I will empower and protect you. Just stand firm and pray, and watch your courage become contagious" (*His Princess, Love Letters from Your King,* Sheri Rose Shepherd).

God has talked to me countless times about holding my head up high. Take courage. "Be strong and courageous! Do not be afraid or terrified of them, for the LORD your God goes with you; He will never leave you nor forsake you" (Deut. 31:6 NIV).

During the times my faith is rocked with another spear coming my way, I hear the Lord say one word. "Remember."

"Remember the wonders He has done, His miracles and the judgments He pronounced" (Ps. 105:5 NIV).

So I do.

I remember the countless times He's shown up, just in time. I remember His faithfulness in fulfilling every promise He's made to me. I remember.

> But recall the former days when, after you were enlightened, you endured a hard struggle with sufferings, sometimes being publicly exposed to reproach and affliction, and sometimes being partners with those so treated. For you had compassion on those in prison, and you joyfully accepted the plundering of your property, since you knew that you yourselves had a better possession and an abiding one. Therefore do not throw away your confidence, which has a great reward. For you have need of endurance, so that when you have done the will of God you may receive what is promised. For, yet a little while, and the coming one will come and will not delay; but my righteous one shall live by faith …
>
> —Hebrews 10:32-38 ESV

Larry Lilly, pastor of Berean Baptist Church in Terre Haute, Indiana, "The Biggest Little Church in the World," wrote, "God often raises up one person, a man or a woman whom God sets on fire with courage and insight and others rally around that person and some sort of great victory results. We've seen this throughout the Bible with Ezekiel, David, Samuel, Deborah, and many more who have stepped forward in courage and made a difference."

God has given me courage. He has raised me up with a fiery passion for His "least of these." Others have rallied around NightShift and me. It has become contagious. And by His grace, He has refined, redeemed, and transformed me to what I am today. A woman of faith.

I asked Him, "Why me? Why did I get to walk this amazing faith-journey with You and NightShift?"

His reply was simple. "I can trust you. You never give up."

I suppose after sharing these stories with you and walking through the memories, I have to agree. I don't give up. NightShift doesn't give up. Ever! There are too many precious lives at stake. At times, when I have felt like giving up, He's taught me to grab the handle of His gigantic sword. His hands cupped over mine. And together we lift and swing the sword of victory, and with a deadly blow, defeat the attacks of the enemy. He's blessed me with an acronym for "sword," and scriptures to stand on when I'm unsteady on my feet.

Surrender! Still! Seek! "Be still and know that I am God" (Ps. 46:10 NIV).

Willing to take the step even when I don't know the outcome. Willing to live by faith. Willing to make mistakes. "Now faith is being sure of what we hope for and certain of what we do not see" (Heb. 11:1 NIV).

Obedient to do what God asks me to do no matter the cost! Don't listen to the lies of the enemy! "We demolish every pretention that sets itself up against the knowledge of God, and we take captive every thought to the obedience of Christ" (2 Cor. 10:5 ESV).

Repent! Radical love! Remember! "… God's kindness leads you towards repentance" (Rom. 2:4 NIV).

Determine not to give up even when times get tough. "The Sovereign Lord is my strength. He makes my feet like feet of a deer. He enables me to go on the heights" (Hab. 3:19 NIV).

In prayer during the writing of this book, our team laid hands on me, asking for God to pour His strength into me to finish well. One dear sister, with her hands placed on my feet, claimed over me, "Put on the full armour of God, so that you can take your stand against the devil's schemes" and take the "sword of the Spirit, which is the word of God" (Eph. 6:11-17 NIV). Britney, my brave assistant, excitedly grabbed a book of poetry that she had written and shared this poem that God had given her recently. Need I say more?

The Sword

You said you had a sword for me
So I walked on to go get it
It was bigger than I thought
But You said You would help with it

We held it strong together
And You whispered in my ear,
These battles aren't for you alone,
Know I'll always be here.
For I know the plans I have for you
And you won't ever be on your own
I'm right behind you here—go on
Take one step forward at a time
For the battle isn't over now
It's only just begun
I've won in eternity's eyes
But here, the fight's still on
So put on your armour-strong
And look into the night
A little fear never hurt anyone
But make sure you keep Me in sight
Walk into the unlit places
And wear My light in love
Fight for freedom, my daughter,
For those who can't see hope
Fight against blindness
For purity
For justice
For truth
For love.

Andy Stanley, *The Principle of the Path: How to Get from Where You Are to Where You Want to Be*, writes, "I concluded with the idea that sometimes God will ask us to do things we don't understand, and that the only way to understand fully is to obey. We will all look back with a sigh of relief or feel the pain of regret." I look back with a huge sigh with relief. Very grateful that He has given me the opportunity and privilege to be His hands and feet! One touch. One hug. One step at a time.

As I tap out these last words, it feels like I've poured my heart and soul into every word. Teardrops. "You keep track of all my sorrows. You have collected all my tears in your bottle. You have recorded each one in your book" (Ps. 56:8 NLT).

Struggling with emotion and an ache in my spirit, sad that these intimate stories have now left me, I feel empty, as if a part of me is gone. This is my love story to my Papa—my Saviour. My labour of love written with the anointing of the Holy Spirit. I feel Him dancing over me singing, "Well done, my daughter!" And a whispered promise, "There are more stories to come. This is not the end. It's just the beginning!"

So I'm happy-sad. Sniff.

DISCUSSION QUESTIONS

1. **Are you ready for the shift?**
   - Are you ready to surrender your life to God?
   - What would your first step be toward the shift?
   - Are you ready?

2. **Are you willing to walk in His strength?**
   - Remember in your own life when you experienced God's strength. How has He held up your head despite what is happening around you and in spite of your fear?
   - Will you hold your head up high and walk with God?

3. **What freedom will you fight for?**
   - Purity?
   - Integrity?
   - Justice?
   - Truth?
   - Love?

4. **What is your love story to God?**

AFTERWORD

THERE ARE SO many people to thank that if I started naming everyone, we would end with a list the size of a small phone book. But one person must be acknowledged for his gracious assistance in the writing and editing of this book, and he is Myles Murchison, a long-time friend, journalist, and author, *The Deathless, Walking In, The Perfect Breadbox, The Year After Custer*.

While we're talking about the book, neither will I forget the eagle-eyes of my faithful editors; Susan Smallwood, Brenda Sasaki, Britney Broadhead and Cynthia Cavanaugh or the design contribution of Tony Mitchell of Original Mix Design, who, by the way, originally created the NightShift logo and branding program for Sisters and the Care Project. Special thanks to Susan Smallwood for her photography skills on the back cover.

And most notably, my three brothers, Mark Sims, Paul Ritchot, and Michael Cash, NightShift's original board members, who walked tirelessly alongside me every step of the way during the early years of the ministry. Without their love, prayers, and dedication, NightShift wouldn't be where it is today.

As I look back over our first seven years, I am in awe of what God has done in my life and in the lives of countless others who have been touched by the ministry. Never in a million years did I imagine that my life would take such a drastic *shift* or that I would experience the magnitude of numerous struggles and victories. In the early days, He told me to dream big—to expect miracles. I didn't realize that He wanted the miracles to begin with me—in me. The *shift* in my own heart had to occur first and gain momentum so His love could ripple out from within me to touch the lives around me. I became part of the miracle.

It wasn't long before I began to urge others to "become part of the miracle" in Whalley. They came and they encouraged others to come. Time and again, I saw the light arise in their hearts—the *shift*—that became a ripple of love that touched the lives around them. It's like the old seventies retro Faberge organic shampoo TV commercial (dating myself again): "You tell two friends, and they'll tell two friends, and so on and so on and so on …"

The circle of waves, this never-ending flow of "love miracles," remains today and will continue to grow as we travel forward into the next era of the ministry.

In the Bible, the number seven symbolizes completeness or perfection. "By the seventh day God completed His work" (Gen. 2:2 NIV). It took Solomon seven years to build the temple in Jerusalem. Not that we built a temple (at times it felt like it), but in many respects, we have completed the first assignment God has given us to reach out to the poor in our city.

As NightShift enters our eighth year, we are mindful of the task that lies ahead. The spears are already striking our footsteps. Number eight is the number of new beginnings, the beginning of a new period. The ark carried eight persons to a new beginning for man on earth (Gen. 7:13). There are seven days in a week; the eighth day begins a new week. As we move forward in our Care Vision in our eighth year with our Cottages and Village, we can't help thinking that it's a new beginning, another exciting era for the ministry.

As this book concludes, it comes with a happy, sad ending. Throughout writing this book, Pastor Steen Laursen was often in my thoughts and heart. Without him and his wife, Lyn, NightShift would not have happened. I expected to receive a telephone call from Pastor Steen as I wrote, for in the past we often laughed together about how, when one of us would think of the other, the other would inevitably call. It happened all the time.

As I reminisced about our humble beginnings in the 2004 snowstorm, snow fell in the Lower Mainland of Vancouver. Coincidence? I paused often and watched huge flakes of snow drifting past my office window and reflected on the early days with Pastor Steen and the Gentle Shepherd.

Pastor Steen must have been thinking of me as I finished my writing because I was thinking of calling him. I wanted to tell him about the book and ask his permission to use his name. Before I could make the call, I received an email from Pastor Steve Witmer: Pastor Steen had gone home to be with the Lord.

An era had come to a close.

My heart is sad. As I wrote about him and the Gentle Shepherd, he lay in a hospital bed battling cancer. If only I had known. I believe he would have gotten a big kick out of knowing that he was in the book. My heart's desire was to honour him as having a key role in the formation of NightShift. It would have been a blessing to tell him this face to face.

So Pastor Steen, as we move forward into our next season of ministry, I sense you smiling. The "love ripples" that you started in the Gentle Shepherd continue to touch lives and gain momentum. I'm sure Papa spoke these words to you as He marshalled you into your heavenly home: "Well done, my good and faithful servant" (Matt. 25:21 NIV).

God promised there were more miracle stories to come.

The next seven-year season of blessings is just beginning.

So until we chat again, "Don't forget to dream about me!"

7 STEPS TOWARD
THE SHIFT

I HAVE A burning desire in my heart to encourage others to experience a paradigm shift in their perception of their fellow men and women, particularly their perception of "the least of these."

I have created seven steps—one step toward this shift for each of the seven years NightShift has been operational. Take any step—preferably more than one step—toward a breathtaking new understanding of yourself and the grace of God.

"A man is never so truly and intensely himself as when he is most possessed by God," wrote clergyman and scholar William Ralph Inge. "It is impossible to say where, in the spiritual life, the human will leaves off and divine grace begins."

I pray God will open eyes and hearts to the suffering and the indignities of those perishing on our streets and those living in poverty in our own backyards. They are our brothers and sisters—the "least of these"—sons and daughters of unnamed parents. Perhaps children of someone you know. Perhaps your own family. People like us looking for hope and purpose.

"We think sometimes that poverty is only being hungry, naked, and homeless. The poverty of being unwanted, unloved, and uncared for is the greatest poverty," said Mother Theresa.

Yes, the "greatest poverty" is not the hunger for food, nor money, nor even the drugs and the objects of obsession. It is the hunger for love. Author John R. Belcher, author of *Helping the Homeless: What About The Spirit of God?* says:

> For many people who are homeless, their disconnectedness from the world is made worse by the actions of the non-homeless. People who are homeless often have strong, unpleasant body odours, may be dirty and unkempt, and exhibit a host of negative physical conditions and actions. Such things are generally offensive to people who might normally approach them about their spiritual needs. Therefore most homeless people are never approached, and their spirituals needs are never addressed. Soup kitchens and shelters may be operated or sponsored by faith-based organizations but very little or any actual time is spent addressing the spiritual needs of the homeless. The homeless are socially shunned and often denied admission to conventional churches or feel unwelcome to do so.

Belcher expounds, "If the transforming power of the Spirit is not offered to the homeless ... people who are homeless may live, but they will live without hope."

We are addressing the "poverty of the soul."

"Blessed are the poor in spirit ..." Jesus speaks to those who are experiencing difficult times and are powerless to change their condition without God. Why does He say that God blesses people when they are poor? "Blessed are the poor in spirit, for theirs is the kingdom of heaven" (Matt. 5:3 NIV).

I began to understand this verse only when I hit the lowest period in my life, became honest with myself, and acknowledged that I was "poor in spirit." When I did, I came to the end of myself and surrendered to God. I began my *shift*.

Up until that point, I wasn't very empathetic. I didn't understand what it meant to walk in a homeless person's shoes or to share in the feelings of his or her sufferings. My first response wasn't empathy; it was apathy or worse, indifference.

When I finally acknowledged my soul poverty, I began to see it reflected back to me in the faces of those suffering on the street. When I stopped navel-gazing, looking at my own self-centeredness, I ceased differentiating between "me and them."

I began to understand compassion. Free Dictionary Online defines compassion as "a feeling of pity and deep awareness of the suffering or misfortune of another coupled with the wish to relieve it." This awareness moved me to God's compassion—from apathy to action—to do something to make a difference in the lives around me, even if it meant only one small act of kindness. "Love your neighbor as yourself" (Matt. 22:39 NIV).

My prayer is that God will tug at your heart for you to become a change-agent in the world around you, even if in some small way. What we do counts. It starts the ripple that streams out to touch others.

Here are seven ways to initiate The Shift.

1. Promote *The Shift*

Yes, I know it sounds a little self-serving, but if the chronicle of my journey and the stories of many others at NightShift has changed your perception of the homeless, then it is likely to change the perception of others. Light exposing our fears and prejudices has a way of dispelling them. Think of yourself as a little like one of the disciples to whom the risen Christ said, "Go ye into all the world, and preach the gospel to every creature" (Mark 16:15 KJV). And if that sounds a little too extreme, think of Robbie Robertson's lyrics in "Shine Your Light."

> Don't wanna be a hero, just an everyday man
> Trying to do the very best job he can.

These days, with access to Twitter, Facebook, and the Internet, spreading the word has never been easier; change has never come more quickly.

2. Donate Clothing

It might not seem like a very important contribution at first glance, but surprisingly, Canadian exports of worn clothes (mostly to India, Pakistan, and Africa)—a business known as "rags" in the trade—were valued at $174 million in 2010, according to the CBC (January 30, 2012), and the business is growing annually.

The rags business is a social enterprise NightShift first looked at in 2009. I brought together a committee to review fundraising options for the collection, processing, and marketing of donated clothing. Our first priority is to ensure that the ministry continues to meet the clothing needs of people living on the street and in poverty. RagTime, as it's called, became a project to utilize excess donated clothing as a means of fundraising. As always, our objective is to raise the maximum amount of funds with the fewest capital and operational expenditures.

Throughout 2010, the committee examined the option of placing clothing donation bins on church and supportive commercial properties. Late in 2011, bins were placed strategically at eight church and two business locations in the Surrey area. Men and women from recovery homes gave back to the community through this initiative, picking up, sorting, and loading clothing under the supervision of a NightShift representative.

Meanwhile, the RagTime team is collaborating and partnering with another ministry in developing a plan to provide mission support to third-world countries in need of microbusiness assistance. The more bins in the community, the greater the revenue potential. Our goal is to eventually secure fifty bins over the next few years. Hard to believe, but fifty bins have the potential to generate enough revenue to support most of NightShift's operational costs.

If you live in the Lower Mainland in British Columbia (or have friends who do), you should know that clothing contributions to the RagTime program will help finance NightShift's street ministries and have some other significant benefits as well.

First, it allows us to continue to be independent of government funding programs. In B.C., community grants are gleaned from the government's gambling revenues: casinos, pub games, online gambling, and lotteries. While it might be lucrative to seek these funds, because we assist people challenged with a myriad of addictions, it just isn't ethical for the ministry to obtain money from the same sources that contribute to the problem.

Our support traditionally comes from the big-heartedness of churches, individuals, the business community, private foundations, and fundraising events. A dependable, sustainable income source like RagTime, however, has been our goal for the past several years and it is close to coming to fruition.

Second, it helps you to be sure your contribution is actually going to charity and not a scam. It's been reported that rag bin pickup is so lucrative than some drivers—notably in Ontario—were reportedly making $12,000 a month and little of the money earned by exporting worn clothing was actually being returned to the charities involved. Our drivers, on the other hand, are non-paid volunteers, most of them our friends in recovery, and 100 percent of all profits are returned to NightShift.

There's even another benefit: just recently, one woman in recovery gave her heart to Jesus in prayer with our RagTime coordinator. God uses every opportunity to shine His light. Hallelujah!

3. Support Sisters

Sisters Thrift Boutique not only helps provide a much needed revenue stream to NightShift but it also provides quality clothing to those in need and brings training and employment opportunities to special needs individuals and people in recovery. Additionally, the business provides areas where volunteers from all walks of life can serve and give back to the community.

Sisters Thrift Boutique's success has been restricted somewhat due to lack of advertising and marketing dollars. Therefore, a creative, cost-effective marketing strategy was developed to take advantage of an affordable online presence and social media such as Twitter and Facebook. Sisters Online came into its own with a new website presence and an exciting, first-of-its-kind Sisters Thrift Store App for smart phones.

I shop till I drop. What a thrill, to shop from my smart phone for great deals, while supporting NightShift. Check it out! You'll be hooked too.

Over the past year, Sisters has become a true extension of NightShift, operating from 10:00 A.M. to 5:00 P.M. when the outreach vehicles are not on the street. In many respects, Sisters has become the "day shift" of NightShift, offering assistance options to various groups. We work with recovery houses to provide clothing and sundry items to the clients and houses. Providing these items, we ensure that clients have the clothing needed to begin their recovery.

Social Services and Surrey Pre-Trial Jail refer clients to Sisters on a regular basis. Upon release, prisoners leave prison with only the meagre items they possessed when incarcerated. Sisters offers free clothing to help former prisoners and social service clients seeking jobs. Presentation being half of the battle when seeking employment, Sisters' assistance makes a tremendous difference in the new job success rate. Sisters also assists young men and women who can't afford the purchase of graduation outfits and continues to support our church partners with their initiatives in providing clothing to single parents.

Sisters and NightShift volunteers sort through donations dropped off at RagTime boxes and remove appropriate clothing needed for the street and store. Clothing donations that have exceeded the inventory needs of NightShift and Sisters are shipped to an international reseller for poundage sales overseas.

Your purchases and contributions directly assist NightShift programs for the homeless and provide opportunities for people making their way into new lives.

4. Volunteer

I know how it can be when you're busy. Sometimes my life feels more corporate than compassionate. I feel I should be in track and field—I'm so adept at jumping hurdles—and sometimes it's all like a blur racing by at lighting speed

Over the past seven years, NightShift has nurtured solid relationships with local agencies. We meet regularly and serve on several committees—the Whalley Integrated Services Team (WIST), Target, Downtown Surrey Business Improvement Association, DTSBIA's Safety Committee, Outreach Workers, and the Surrey Homeless and Housing Task Force. We're included in the recent release of the

City of Surrey Crime Reduction Report Card, which speaks volumes about the City of Surrey's acceptance of this ministry. It all consumes lots of our time but keeps us involved and informed, and when I wonder why I keep leaping the hurdles, all I have to do is go back on the street with the other volunteers. The reason I'm involved with NightShift all makes sense again.

Throughout this book, I've talked about the impact of the *shift*—not only on those whom NightShift has reached—but also the impact on my own soul. It is an experience that changed my life. I'm not much of a crime fiction reader, but a friend showed me this passage from novelist James Lee Burke's book, *Pegasus Descending*, that looks at the struggle of people in duress from a somewhat different slant:

> ... A sergeant in my platoon who had served in World War II, Korea, and Vietnam told me he was the wisest man he had ever known.

> "Why's that?" I asked.

> "Because I've spent a lifetime seeing people in duress," he replied.

> "So?" I said.

> "That's when the best and worst of people come out. When they're in duress. Most of the time the best comes out."

Volunteering with NightShift or with any group that reaches out to the homeless—getting your hands dirty—can become the most rewarding, transformative experience of your life … being there and witnessing *the best coming out*.

Come to one of our information sessions. Take a test drive. You'll discover you're not alone. More and more churches are coming on board and every month we see approximately forty new faces gracing our doorstep to volunteer. If you need an invitation, a little nudge toward the *shift*, this is it. Take it. See what it can do for you.

5. Contribute Financially

Not everyone can volunteer, but your financial donations and gifts-in-kind are gratefully received by NightShift. We estimate that the combined value of financial gifts, volunteer hours, and gift-in-kind items exceeds $1.5 million each year, and here's what they support:

Our Outreach Program continues to serve those on the street, with new churches and volunteers joining the ranks on a regular basis. We opened an emergency shelter with the Extreme Weather program. We have recently launched a NightShift Homeless Soccer Team to compete with other homeless soccer teams locally, offering our street friends the opportunity to have fun with a purpose and to integrate on a different level with volunteers and the community.

The Care Centre stepped into its own with licensed contract and intern counsellors and a prayer ministry team on board. Clients come from a variety of walks of life. Some are homeless, some formerly homeless; most are financially struggling, many are on parole or awaiting trial. Referrals come from other local service agencies and from the church community. Most of our clients can't afford the going rate ($70-$110 per session) because they are on a low or fixed income or do not have an extended health care plan. The sliding scale is really needed and appreciated. It ensures no one is turned away. Contract counsellors bring their own clients and pay a percentage of their rate for the use of the counselling room. The Care Centre also rents space to a community-based reintegration program designed to support people newly released from prison who have been convicted of sex offences, admit to committing these offences, and request help to prevent further offending.

The Care Vision further expanded with the launch of our Care Bus, formerly known as the Isaiah 61 Truck. Nurses, dentists, dental hygienists, counsellors, and RCMP met several months in round-table discussions and focus groups to help identify operational details.

The Care Bus vision is to reach those who would not be able to access community services otherwise. We are networking with recovery homes and shelters to bring counselling services to men and women in recovery, who are unable to utilize our Care Centre due to high relapse rates. Currently under examination is the need for service to seniors who are housebound and unable to access counselling, nursing, or dental care independently.

We are in discussion with dentists and their governing body, and it is only a matter of time before dental care is provided on the Care Bus. The plan is for volunteer dentists and hygienists to provide basic dental screening and basic dental care and education services on the Care Bus, and to provide more complicated dental procedures with a local dental office. The Care Bus offers referral information to recovery homes and social services and will soon offer a library service.

And, of course, we are expanding our recovery program to include a Care Village in Fort St. John.

That is the benefit we receive from your contribution. The benefits you receive for giving to God's work—bringing sustenance, hope, and love to the homeless—are clearly stated in His Word. "Honour the Lord with your substance and with the first fruits of all your produce; then your barns will be filled with plenty, and your vats will be bursting with wine" (Prov. 3:9-10 NIV). "Some give freely, yet grow all the richer; others withhold what is due and only suffer want. A generous person will be enriched, and one who gives water will get water" (Prov. 11:24-25 NIV).

6. Pray

"The greatest tragedy of life is not unanswered prayer, but unoffered prayer," wrote F. B. Meyer, a Baptist minister who served inner-city missions in London at the turn of the twentieth century.

We ask that your prayers *not* be unoffered.

We ask that you pray for us, for our success in reaching the people on the street who want to return to their families, and for those who want to rise up to a new life.

Pray, like Jonah, in gratitude and thanks for God's redemptive power. "… But you, Lord my God brought my life up from the pit. When my life was ebbing away, I remembered you, Lord, and my prayer rose to you, to your holy temple" (Jonah 2: 6-7 NIV).

Pray, like Solomon, that all of us at NightShift are clear in our understanding of the needs and aspirations of the homeless people we encounter. "Therefore give to Your servant an understanding heart to judge Your people, that I may discern between good and evil" (1 Kings 3:9 NKJV).

Pray, like Job, with the certainty and knowledge of God's will. "I know that You can do all things; no purpose of Yours can be thwarted" (Job 42:2 NIV).

We believe in the power of prayer. And as a church lawn sign once announced: All Prayers Gratefully Received.

7. Smile

What would it look like if we all did our part? One small random act of kindness. Sometimes offering the power of the "Spirit of God" is as simple as radiating a smile to another. A nod, an acknowledgment that a homeless person is seen by another and not with scorn. Seen by you as a person loved by God.

What would your life look like if you could *shift* from comfortable and cross the line to the unknown? Love a person living on the street unconditionally? Provide hope and maybe help him or her find purpose?

I know this sounds idealistic. But imagine the impact this would have in the world if we did this. If this book spurs you on do to something out of the ordinary, I'll be one happy girl!

At the end of life we will not be judged by how many diplomas we have received, how much money we have made, how many great things we have done. We will be judged by: I was hungry, and you gave me something to eat, I was naked and you clothed me. I was homeless, and you took me in. Hungry, not only for bread but hungry for love. Naked, not only for clothing but naked of human dignity and respect. Homeless not only for want of a room of bricks—but homeless because of rejection. This is Christ in distressing disguise.

—Mother Teresa

God, give us a heart of compassion and eyes to see the needs of our fellow man—the obvious ones we see on the streets of our city and the not-so-obvious ones who sit beside us in the pews of our own church. Lord, give us the hands and feet of action to do something in some small way to make a difference in the world around us.

One soul at a time. One ripple at a time.

Amen.

TESTIMONIALS

W E'RE NOT JUST a soup kitchen helping street people struggling with substance abuse and mental health challenges. We are an organization made up of people from all walks of life, gender, age, ethnicity, and demographics. We are hearts coming together—to love and be loved, to serve and be served.

"Even the rich are hungry for love, for being cared for, for being wanted, for having someone to call their own," said Mother Teresa.

I know intimately how God changed my heart on the street.

"Sometimes we think we are bringing Jesus with us when we as Christians do volunteer work with the poor and the homeless. When in actuality you are going to meet Jesus when you rub elbows with the poor and the homeless."

This profound statement is not mine. I don't know who the author is, but I use it because it really impacts my heart.

It speaks the truth. I came to Whalley thinking I would make a difference there, but in reality the difference started in me. God changed my heart through the process. *The shift.*

Our mission statement states, "NightShift's mission is to love unconditionally and help others find hope and purpose." NightShift is a place for people to gather, to find hope in their own lives and a purpose to continue on, even in the tough times. Mother Teresa said, "Being unwanted, unloved, uncared for, forgotten by everybody, I think that is a much greater hunger, a much greater poverty than the person who has nothing to eat. We must find each other."

Let others tell you their stories.

A letter from a team leader who responded to God's call:

When I saw the NightShift video announcement at our church looking for volunteers, I realized this was a great opportunity for missions work in my own backyard and to minister to the homeless. I wanted to do my part. I've now been with NightShift for four years and have been tremendously blessed through this ministry. It is true that the more you give, the more you get. The love and dedication of the volunteers is awe-inspiring. Seeing and hearing how lives have been changed through this ministry is the fuel that keeps me going.

Volunteers have revelations about life. A letter from a volunteer:

At first, I was a little nervous. I wondered what I would say to the people we served. It seemed like our worlds were so far apart. As I began to get to know a few regulars it seemed as if the Lord impressed upon my heart that only a few unwise decisions, only a few bad circumstances, only a few missteps, only a few missed opportunities separated our worlds. I could see firsthand what drug and alcohol addiction did to people's physical, emotional, and spiritual state. I could see how mental illness could take someone down a hopeless path. I witnessed what the working poor have to do to make the money go further.

People see the change that love creates. A letter from another volunteer:

There was a party in heaven last Friday night! I just expected to tell anyone who seemed interested about NightShift Street Ministries and what we do. It was Missions Fest and I was excited to meet like-hearted believers all under the same roof. As the night wore on, the flow of people by booth slowed down. I think it was around 8 P.M. when I heard a young man's voice nearby.

"NightShift again?"

"Again?" I asked, wondering if he wasn't pleased at our presence. "How do you mean?"

"Well," he began, "if it wasn't for NightShift, I'd be dead. You see, this one night I was on the street and I had planned on killing myself that night … Just wanted to put an end to it. And then someone from NightShift came up and talked to me. They gave me some good food and I felt so much better. Like someone cared, you know. So I didn't follow through with my plans."

Wow! I thought. I asked his name and told him how glad I was to meet him.

"I'm Shaun ... So yeah ... Here I am again and it's funny ... I'm in pain again...." Pointing to the NightShift logo on my T-shirt, he continued, "... and here is NightShift. Again!"

He went on to tell me that he was six months clean on Wednesday and had to have all his upper teeth pulled. He had been in so much pain and was tempted to go back and numb it the way he always had. Using drugs. But since he saw us, he just knew he'd make it through just fine. He said he wasn't sure "how all this crazy stuff happens and how, like, NightShift just happens to be involved again."

"I do," I said. "Do you believe in God, Shaun?"

"Oh, yes. Of course."

"He has a purpose and plan for each of us and He is involved in the smallest details of our lives ... do you know about Jesus?"

"Oh, yeah ... He's the Son of God ... He died on a cross to save everyone ..."

"So are you a Christian?"

"No. I don't think so ..."

So I went on to fill in the blanks and expand a bit on the most amazing love story of all time. The story of how "God so loved the world, that He gave his only begotten Son so that whoever believes in Him should not perish but have everlasting life."

"Do you believe that, Shaun?"

"Yes ..." he said softly, overcome with emotion.

I asked him if he would pray aloud with me and ask Jesus to forgive him and be his Lord and Saviour. He answered with a resounding yes. So just like that, at a booth in Canada Place, Shaun made Jesus Christ Lord of his life. After we prayed, he gave me a huge hug! Three actually.

"Thank you! Thank you so much! I'm a Christian now ... That's amazing!"

"Yes, you are, brother! Welcome to the family! I'd love to have you come to church with us ..."

"I would too ... I will call you."

And then there was rejoicing in the heavens in the presence of the angels of God. What a party that must have been!

Others see the opportunities the Lord provides. Another letter:

A new senior pastor prepared for a Sunday message by giving each one in attendance a jigsaw puzzle piece, and had us write "I fit" on the back. He went on to say in his message that every one of God's people had a purpose and gifting that made them fit somewhere in His plans. This encouraged me and made me a little sad. That all changed after my husband encouraged me to get involved in a street mission work called NightShift. After being unsure, apprehensive, and just uncomfortable with the idea, I went. I went to an empty field, in the worst part of town, where an old truck and some beat-up tables were drawing a crowd.

I stood amongst the people and saw the love that was being shared that night. I realized two wonderful things. That same love, the love of God, was drawing me. "I fit, right here!" I didn't have to cross an ocean or hike into wherever to help others. God had opened a wonderful opportunity for me to help others right in my own backyard, like He planned it!

From an AOK leader and NightShift staff member, who writes about her night on the street with one of our youth and young adult teams:

To provide the context, our team walks the designated route, handing out hot chocolate, and we usually stop by the skate park to hang out with the youth there for a bit. We all pour hot chocolates, sit, and chat. On this night, we sat down with a group of young guys and asked if we could pray before we left. They all seemed really responsive and one guy spoke out and shared about his mom's state of health, saying she'd been on medication for seventeen years. Recently she had to have surgery, which she was finding so hard to handle. He was really upset and wanted us to pray for anything to help the situation. So we joined him and pleaded with God to step in. Two weeks later, we saw the group again. After some conversation, someone asked the guy we'd connected with before how his mom was doing. In response his eyes lit up.

"Dude," he said, "my mom is totally healed! She is completely off medication after seventeen years. It's a miracle. God answered your prayers. Thank you."

I was shocked and couldn't help almost crying on the spot when I heard that. I know that some of our street friends embellish stories that are the reality of addiction; but this guy was different. God used the innocence of a young man to show that He hears our prayers and answers them. Even in my doubt, I had to believe this story!

Sometime it feels like I just go hand out some hot chocolate, have a conversation, sometimes pray, and then move on ... but there is more. We do those things, but God stays He swirls around wherever we move, whomever we talk to, and He lingers after. It's beautiful and I'm so grateful that God moved the curtain that night. We got to see a bit of His plan in the life of this son and his mom. He's moving beyond the nights we go out. He finishes every conversation we start and has the power to continue to spiritually "feed" His children beyond our hot chocolate and muffins. Those little glimpses of answered prayers provide hope and purpose to keep on us going, keep serving, and most importantly, keep loving the people God puts in our way. He will do the rest.

A letter from a beloved street friend whom I met the night of the snowstorm:

I've known MaryAnne for a long time and was involved with NightShift from the very beginning. My belief in the Lord became more intense and life became more pure being around my Christian friends at NightShift. It feels good to cry within and cry out loud. My life is smoother being with down-to-earth people. The Lord became easier to understand. True Christians know how to relate to people and speak in plain English. My heart cried for many nights over my wife. Christian people have helped turn me around. As I got to know these Christian people better, I realized it was because of our Lord Jesus Christ.

I am wearing my lion mask today to make me feel more relaxed. One must be consistent, true to you, and true to the Lord. My Christian friends give me hope with all my heart. I have said no to drugs and have been clean for three to four days now. I want to stay clean from the hard drugs. I feel good about myself today. The Lord says stand stern and not to rebuke the street people in anger. The Lord does not want us to retaliate against these people who have hurt me.

Last but not least—bittersweet—a letter from a former street friend:

I am only wishing to extend my gratitude to you at this time. It has been many years since I received help from your organization; my intention is to let you know that you have made a difference in my life. It was with your help that I was able to eventually find my way out of a life of addiction and pain. Through the daily kindness and understanding which I was shown at your food truck, I was able to finally rally the strength to get off the street and begin the journey back to a life of honesty and sobriety.

There are no words that can illustrate the magnitude of the effect that your kindness has had for me. I can only say that I feel indebted to the many people whose daily efforts to help and care for the many destitute people in Whalley is an inspiration to me. I see it as an example of humanity in its highest form, there can be no greater gift than the hope and relief that your blessed organization has shown to so many. The non-judgmental, open-handed generosity given to many others and me was instrumental in restoring my faith in humanity, I was a person who believed that the world was a cruel and heartless place; it was my belief that no one gave a #@$% about anyone. I was without hope.

The example of your organization and the many people whose open dedication and genuine love for their fellow man has shown me that there is goodness and love in the hearts of people. By witnessing this, I slowly began to believe that perhaps the world and my life within it has a higher purpose. It was through this realization that my spirit was once again awakened. I was able to understand

and see that living from the heart was not weak or foolish but actually the way to peace for my own battered spirit. So thank you.

My words seem less than adequate to impart how truly wonderful your love for people is. Thank you and thank God for His presence in all the people who work with you.

Finally, I wanted to say on a more personal note that there is one lady there who stands out in my memory; I believe she is known as Sister? I cannot recall her name; however, she is a kind woman with blond or light-colored hair. Several years ago, she went very far out of her way to help my girlfriend. I remember her well for her kindness. It is, however, her commitment to the people which I wish to acknowledge. This lady made attempts to help my girlfriend; this was not an easy task. Both of us were very needy and hard cases, full of deception and callous in our attitudes and actions. This lady walked alongside of our shortcomings, looking past them and seeking only to help. It was with her open heart that I was able to back away from my own sense of commitment to my girlfriend and concentrate on taking care of myself.

Sadly, my girlfriend never made it; she died. I honestly believe that it would have happened much sooner had it not been for this lady's several attempts to rescue her. I also want to point out that at the time of her death, she had been clean for almost ninety days, the first time in her life she had ever been able to find any peace and it all started from the help we received from this lady. Sadly, she relapsed while living in a recovery centre and died of an overdose. It was, however, still a triumph as she had made peace with her family and most importantly, herself.

Again, thank you, thank God for people such as you.

People's lives impacted by the love of others. Mother Teresa sums it up perfectly, "Let us touch the dying, the poor, the lonely, and the unwanted according to the graces we have received and let us not be ashamed or slow to do the humble work."

WHAT NOW?

Volunteering

THERE ARE MANY WAYS TO SERVE AT NIGHTSHIFT. NightShift relies on support of all kinds and encourages volunteers to come forward to be trained to cook, serve meals, sort and give out clothes, share time and conversation with our street friends, drive our ministry vehicles, lend a hand in the warehouse, provide administrative support, help organize fundraising events or assist with the various outreach programs.

START WITH INFORMATION. NightShift welcomes individuals or groups (adult or youth) to find out more about the ministry by attending an informal Information Night. This is part of the mandatory training program if an individual goes on to volunteer with NightShift.

Donating

IF YOU ARE MOVED TO TAKE ACTION, but are unable to volunteer, there are other ways to give.

- ✓ *Pray.* Remember us in your prayers especially those we serve and love on the street.

- ✓ *Financially.* Every penny counts. Your one-time gift or monthly donation is greatly appreciated.

- ✓ *Gift-in-kind.* Help keep our warehouse stocked by donating much-needed food, supplies, blankets or clothing.

- ✓ *Sponsorship.* Sponsor a nightly meal to help one of our outreach teams serve hot food or support one of our fundraising events.

- ✓ *Leave a Legacy.* Planned giving through your estate can benefit a charity of your choosing into the future.

- ✓ *Gift.* Share The Shift book with someone you love.

Check our website www.nightshiftministries.org for more information or email info@nightshiftministries.org with any questions.

NEXT STEP

Prayer of Surrender

DO YOU BELIEVE IN GOD? If so, do you believe His promises, His Word? Have you surrendered your life to Him? If you would like a personal relationship with God, pray this simple prayer of surrender:

> *"God, I know that in my lifetime, I have not always lived for You and I have sinned in ways I probably don't even know. I know that You have plans for me and I want to live in those plans.*
>
> *I pray to You for forgiveness for the ways in which I have sinned. I am choosing now to accept Jesus into my heart. I am eternally grateful for His sacrifice on the Cross and how He died so I can have eternal life.*

I pray that I be filled with the Holy Spirit and that I will live as You desire me to live. I will strive to overcome temptations and not let sin control me.

I put myself in Your hands. I pray that You will work in my life and guide my steps so that I continue to live for You.

In Your name I pray. Amen"

Name _____

Date _____

NOW DO THIS:

1. Go tell someone that you just accepted Jesus into your heart!

2. Find yourself a Bible-believing church where you can learn more about God.

3. Read the Bible starting with the Gospel of John.

4. Share your 'shift' story with me at: www.maryanneconnor.com

5. Connect with us at www.nightshiftministries.org if you
   need more prayer or want to share the joy and love
   that God has just deposited into your heart! We'd love
   to hear from you.

MaryAnne Connor Rev, RPC
Founder/President

NightShift Street Ministries
10635 King George Boulevard, Surrey, BC V3T 2X6
Office 604.953.1114   Fax 604.953.1415

EMBRACE THE SHIFT

By
Kelita

THE FIRST TIME I MET MARYANNE, I witnessed her compassionate spirit for her organization, NightShift Street Ministries. Then I read her book, *The Shift – The Power of Belief.* Wow!

I read with eagerness, hanging onto every word. I cried, I cheered. I felt her growing pains as she birthed her life's calling. Something inside me ignited! I had been deeply touched and inspired. With everything inside of me I knew I had to write a song that might embody this incredible woman and the heart of everything her ministry encompassed.

The Holy Spirit and I began collaborating and soon *Embrace The Shift* was born.

After a generous donor came forward, we recorded the song. Whitewater Studio and some of Vancouver's top musicians and producers also gave willingly to the cause.

What a privilege and honour it is for me to release *Embrace The Shift* alongside a generous and loving organization like NightShift Street Ministries.

The Lyrics

No more pain and no more sorrow
Or feeling sorry for myself
When I look into the mirror
I can see somebody else

Nobody said it would be easy
So many battles to be won
But we can never place a price tag
On the life of each precious one

Chorus
Oh I know you must feel like you're all alone
But there's a love that runs deep
Where you can always find a home
Open the door
To your heart
Receive the gift
And embrace the shift

You and I can make a difference
To the very least of these
I know that anything is possible
When I'm surrendered down on my knees

He could be your brother
She might be your sister
It could be your mother
Love is the way that we heal one another

Embrace the Shift is available as a 99¢ download on iTunes.
Partial profits go to NightShift Street Ministries. Makes an
inspiring gift.

ENDNOTES

Chapter 1:

John Ortberg, *If You Want to Walk on Water, You Have to Get Out of the Boat*, Grand Rapids, Michigan, Zondervan, 2000.

Chapter 3:

Josh Wilson, *Before the Morning*, released on the album, *Life is Not a Snapshot* (2010).

Hannah Hurnard, *Hinds' Feet on High Places*, England, Christian Literature Crusade, 1955.

Chapter 5:

The Commodores, *The Nightshift*, from the album, *Nightshift* (1985).

Chapter 6:

Randy Newman, *It's Money That I Love*, from the album, *Born Again* (1979).

Chapter 7:

Kevin Diakiw, *The Surrey Leader*, 2004.
Myles Murchison, *BC Business Magazine*, Vancouver, B.C., October 2004.
Andrew Holota, *The Surrey Leader*, April 2004.

Chapter 8:

Kevin Diakiw, *The Surrey Leader*, September & December 2004.
Brennan Manning, *The Ragamuffin Gospel*, Sisters, Oregon, Multnomah Publishing, 2000.

Chapter 9:

Leonardo Boff, Brazilian theologian and writer and leader in the Liberation Theology movement, *Church: Charism and Power: Liberation Theology and the Institutional Church.*
David Shive, *Night Shift; God Works in Dark Hours of Life,* Lincoln, Nebraska, Back to the Bible Publishing, 2001.
Gene Edwards, *A Tale of Three Kings*, Goleta, California, Christian Books, 1980.
The Surrey Leader, December 2004 (December 1 & 7th, 2 separate articles).
Kent Spencer, *The Province Newspaper*, December, 2004.
Ted Colley, *The Surrey Now Newspaper*, December 11, 2004.

Chapter 10:

Kevin Diakiw, *The Surrey Leader*, June 2004.

Dr. Abraham Maslow, American professor of psychology whose model, Maslow's Hierarchy of Needs, a theory of self actualization, examines the five needs every human being requires for a fulfilled and puposeful existence. http://www.vectorstudy.com/management_theories/maslows_hierarchy_of_needs.htmaccessed September 1, 2012.

Chapter 11:

Kent Spencer, The Province Newspaper, December 2004.

Dr. Seuss, *How the Grinch Stole Christmas*, New York, Random House, 1957.

Marisa Babic, *The Surrey Now*, January 26, 2005.

Kevin Diakiw, *The Surrey Leader*, January 23, 2004.

John Bevere, *The Bait of Satan*, Lake Mary, Florida, Charisma House, 2004.

Chapter 13:

Marisa Babic, *The Surrey Now*, March 2005.

Chapter 14:

Andy Park is a dear friend, a worship leader, a creative and down to earth pastor who has created some of the most incredible music that reflects the heart of our Papa God. This song, *Wonder Working God,* is a favorite and can be found on the self-same album entitled, *Wonder Working God*, released in June, 2009.

Chapter 15:

This quote from Dianne Watts, now Mayor of the City of Surrey, can be found at http://en.wikipedia.org/wiki/Dianne_Watts, accessed September 1, 2012.

This adaptation is of course from the classic 1989 movie, *Field of Dreams,* where the character, Ray Kinsella, hears a voice that says, "If you build it, he will come, referring to a baseball diamond. http://en.wikipedia.org/wiki/Field_of_Dreams accessed September 1, 2012.

Chapter 16:

E.B. White (1899-1985), http://www.quotesdaddy.com/quote/1397769/e-b-white/before-the-seed-there-comes-the-thought-of-bloom accessed September 1, 2012.

Drs. Michael Krausz & Iris Torchalla, Healing Homelessness, https://www.helpstpauls.com/wp-content/uploads/2012/08/Healing-Homelessness.pdf, accessed September 1, 2012

Chapter 17:

Rate of Return, http://en.wikipedia.org/wiki/Rate_of_return accessed September 1, 2012.

The most recent statistics on federal inmate costs in Canada http://www.torontosun.com/2012/02/28/it-costs-113000-a-year-to-lodge-a-federal-prisoner-report, accessed September 1, 2012.

Chapter 18:

All of Joyce Meyers Resources can be found on her website,http://www.joycemeyer.org/home.aspx, accessed September 1, 2012.

Andy Stanley, *Making Vision Stick*, Grand Rapids, Michigan, Zondervan, 2007.

Kevin Diakiw, *The Surrey Now*, Sept 2007.

Chapter 20:

Willie Nelson, *On the Road Again,* as part of the soundtrack for the movie and album, both entitled, Honeysuckle Rose (1980).

Chapter 21:

Kevin Diakiw, *The Surrey Leader*, January 12, 2012.

Dr. Neil T. Anderson, *Discipleship Counselling*, Ventura, California, Regal, 2003.

Chapter 22:

This beloved, well known anthem of surrender and honor is attributed to Laurie Klein http://createdtoworship. multiply.com/journal/item/18/Laurie-Kleins-I-Love-You-Lord?&show_interstitial=1&u=%2Fjournal%2Fit emaccessed September 1, 2012.

Chapter 23:

Sheri Rose Shepherd, *His Princess, Love Letters From Your King*, Sisters, Oregon, Multnomah Publishing, 2004.

Larry Lilly is a passsionate follower of God, a pastor at Berean Baprist Church in Terre Haute Indiana, http://www.bbcth.com/ as well as a blogger, http://www.larrylilly.net/index.html, accessed September 1, 2012.

"The Sword", an original poem inspirationally created and included with gracious permission from Ms. Britney Broadhead, my former assistant.

Andy Stanley, *The Principle of the Path, How to Get From Where You Are to Where You Want to Be*, Nashville, Tennessee, Thomas Nelson, 2008.

7 Steps Towards The Shift:

Mother Teresa, (1910-1997) "We think sometimes that poverty is only being hungry, naked and homeless. The poverty of being unwanted, unloved, and uncared for is the greatest poverty. http://www.brainyquote.com/quotes/quotes/m/mothertere130839.html

John R. Belcher & Frederick A. DiBlasio, *Helping the Homeless: Where Do We Go From Here?* Lexington, Massachusetts, Lexington Books, 1990.

Free dictionary online http://www.thefreedictionary.com/ accessed September 1, 2012.

News story about the clothing donation programs across the country and controversy and challenges that come with it http://www.cbc.ca/news/canada/story/2012/01/26/charity-clothing-bins-millions.htmlaccessed September 1, 2012.

James Lee Burke, *Pegasus Descending,* New York, Simon & Shuster, 2006.

F. B.Meyer (1847-1929) "The greatest tragedy of life is not unanswered prayer, but unoffered prayer." http://christian-quotes.ochristian.com/F.B.-Meyer-Quotes/ accessed September 1, 2012.

Mother Teresa, (1910-1997), "At the end of life we will not be judged by how many diplomas we have received, how much money we have made, how many great things we have done.We will be judged by "I was hungry, and you gave me something to eat, I was naked and you clothed me. I was homeless, and you took me in. Hungry not only for bread, but hungry for love. Naked, not only for clothing, but naked of human dignity and respect. Homeless not only for want of a room of bricks – but homeless because of rejection. This is Christ in distressing disguise." http://www.goodreads.com/quotes/759-at-the-end-of-life-we-will-not-be-judged accessed September 1, 2012.

Mother Teresa, (1910-1997), "Even the rich are hungry for love, for being cared for, for being wanted, for having someone to call their own." http://www.brainyquote.com/quotes/quotes/m/mothertere103103.html accessed September 1, 2012.

Mother Teresa, (1910-1997), "Being unwanted, unloved, uncared for, forgotten by everybody, I think that is a much greater hunger, a much greater poverty than the person who has nothing to eat. We must find each other." http://www.brainyquote.com/quotes/quotes/m/mothertere158109.html accessed September 1, 2012.

Testimonials:

Mother Teresa, (1910-1997), "Let us touch the dying, the poor, the lonely and the unwanted according to the graces we have received and let us not be ashamed or slow to do the humble work. http://www.brainyquote.com/quotes/authors/m/mother_teresa.html accessed September 1, 2012.